Right Fit Leading

Right Fit Leading

Emotionally Intelligent Team Building

Michael A. Brown Sr., PhD

Right Fit Communications LLC

CONTENTS

Right Fit Leading:
Emotionally Intelligent Team Building

By Dr. Michael A. Brown Sr., PhD

ABSTRACT: ***The Right Fit Leading (RFL) Process*** offers help and education for companies and learning institutions to develop leaders and teams. ***RFL*** focuses training on all members, because you cannot develop leaders by only focusing on the person in charge and what they need to do or to improve on. Using Leader-Member Exchange (LMX) Theory based in part on an article by Fred Dansereau, George Graen, and William Haga (1975), you can understand that leadership development is best done collaboratively. Skill development, then, is best done by creating relationships as an integral part of the training. This is non-traditional, because the "normal" process is to train the leader. Then, the leader trains or motivates the team to follow. Collaboratively developing the skills that the leader and those they lead delivers shared understanding and effective team building. This is the challenge that is addressed in this work.

List of Figures

This book is the next major step in my continuing evolution as a leader and as a developer of leaders. For many years, I developed myself and others in a variety of ways. I went from directing, to motivating, to collaborating, to innovating, and then I did it all over again.

There are two factors in my personal development that make this book possible. The first is the way I was trained as a leader in the U.S. Air Force. I spent 24 years perfecting my craft, finally rising to the highest enlisted rank before retiring in 2000. I retired as a chief master sergeant, a rank held by only one percent of the active-duty force at any one time. I served as

public affairs advisor to two chief master sergeants of the Air Force, the highest-ranking enlisted member of that service. I finished my career as the public affairs career field manager, advising the director of Air Force Public Affairs on the morale, welfare, and proper utilization of about 1,000 journalists, broadcasters, and bandsmen.

The second factor in my personal development was coaching high school football after I left the Air Force. I continued to hone my leadership style and, eventually, captured it in my 2021 book, *3D Coaching: Suggestions for a New Approach*. I formalized 3D, which is dedication, detail, and discipline, to characterize my leadership philosophy. This is how I lead and follow every day.

Capturing the essence of 3D led to the creation of ***The Right Fit Leading (RFL) Process***. After I published ***3D Coaching***, I took a longer look at what it provides that can help others. To ensure it was a process that could be used in any leader or team development situation, I added capabilities to arrive at ***RFL***. The second capability, ***RAMP*** (relate, anticipate, motivate, participate), demonstrates the inspiration to create beneficial relationships. Then, I added ***CLUE*** (connect, listen, understand, and engage), which is a method to motivate ourselves and others to take on challenges that we might not attempt otherwise.

3D is the foundation of ***The RFL Process***. My *3D* philosophy begins with dedication to a team or to a task. It requires paying attention to detail and doing whatever is required to make sure each task is done correctly. If it is not done correctly, retrain or redo to get it right. We must also always be disciplined, whether we are talking about family, school, team rules, or personal accountability. *3D* teaches us to learn, listen, and engage.

Dedication is about what we believe in life. We much search our soul and examine our fundamental belief in life and love and faith. This is what guides our lives, and we must dedicate ourselves to those values. If we fail to do this, we tend to struggle in life.

It is important to find a fit between your personal values and those of the team. Every day, we face challenges and decisions that require our values to determine the best way to proceed. When the team fits your values, you tend to make decisions on the fly and success comes easy. This fit allows you to see the value in participating in the team construct. It allows you to align your personal goals with team goals. Of course, there will be times when your goals do not exactly align with the team, but this is where engagement and feedback are important. A good fit between your values and team values certainly helps.

If there is a disconnect between personal values and team values, stress is created. People may have difficulty making the decisions required. This is counterproductive for everyone because it can create a struggle to do the things the team needs because they may go against personal values.

There are certainly times when conflict is good. For instance, when the leader changes or if you change teams, there will be an adjustment period to match to new values and expectations. This transition can be healthy if everyone stays engaged to help the changes take place. Always remember that changes in team members and administrative aspects of the team are challenging in terms of maintaining team momentum and organizational balance. Still, **Dedication** requires commitment to giving heart and soul in pursuit of achieving and maintaining that balance.

The second "D" is **Detail**, which is about working "where the rubber meets the road." Attention to detail requires that everyone work hard on developing their skills and on perfecting their craft. All team members top to bottom must be open to learning new things and improving skills at every opportunity. Do not be satisfied with today's performance, even if today brought rewards in one form or another.

The journey to success is constant, and we must continue to pursue it. Avoid becoming satisfied with the most recent success. Celebrate successes, of course, but then find your way back to the focus and effort that delivered that success. Continued hard work keeps you on top, or at least keeps you hungry to strive for the next recognition.

Strive for accuracy in all things and be ready to confront risks to your success. Identify, analyze, and quantify the risks in your team so you can work to eliminate or mitigate them. Work towards a state of perfection by identifying the tasks needed to succeed and working through them methodically. Use repetition to make task accomplishment a habit.

Detail is about using effective listening skills to create great communication. Take all the time that is required to achieve the desired outcomes. Keep in mind that preparation, planning, and design are the keys to setting up practices that matter and that move you and your team toward improved performance.

Leaders and teams need to listen to each other about what they are experiencing as they learn and practice their skills. Allow anyone to question what is going on and to suggest ways they want to approach things that are difficult for them. It is not necessary for everyone to agree, but it is crucial that everyone listens. This sparks appreciation and confidence and can lead to acceptance. Even when we think someone is saying something that is not directly relevant, we should take some time to listen anyway. We may find that they are reaching out about an issue that is causing them stress or that they do not understand. Taking this time to listen will build trust with people and, in turn, they will not be afraid to come to you if they have a problem.

Discipline, the third "D", is characterized in three types: preventative, supportive, and corrective. Preventative discipline explains the actions taken before an undesirable behavior to stop it from happening. Supportive discipline explains the actions taken to help a person reshape or redirect their own behavior. Corrective discipline explains the actions taken as a consequence of undesirable behavior.

When we talked about **Dedication** and **Detail** earlier, we discussed methods that should guide team-friendly actions in the process of taking care of preventative discipline. We can limit or eliminate undesirable behaviors and make corrective discipline unnecessary through the interactive engagements we are discussing.

The **Discipline** that we use in the *3D* philosophy is supportive. It motivates leaders and those they lead to discover their potential and set a course to continued success. Being supportive means leaders and teams are open to changing strategies or techniques to be sure they are capturing everyone's attention and motivation. In interactive sessions, be supportive of each other by showing interest in someone's life beyond the job (without getting too personal). When someone is struggling to learn or master a skill, use eye contact or change your physical proximity with them to demonstrate commitment.

Sometimes suggesting other ways to do a task can help. You can also work with small challenges that break the major task into smaller parts that may be more manageable. In a team setting, you might let someone continue to work on a skill or task while the rest of the group moves to the next step. All of these approaches have the ability to take the spotlight off of any member's struggle, at least for the moment. Supportive Discipline encourages everyone to find what works best for them. This variation may separate the team a bit, but it allows each member to get stronger. The result should be a stronger team.

Developing *3D, RAMP,* and *CLUE* into *The RFL Process* is valuable to leader and team development going forward. Beliefs, values, challenges, decisions, competition, fit, conflict, adjustment, transition, alignment, commitment, balance, skills, learning, performance, achievement, accuracy, risk, preparation, communication, practice, perfection, demonstration, trust, behavior, supportive, potential, success, strategy, plan, and technique are all involved. These are the keys to our use of *RFL*. They represent avenues to success that result from healthy communication within the team, a shared understanding of the skills that lead to success, and a commitment to the behaviors that support individuals and the team equally.

The RFL Process can be applied in any organizational setting and with any team of any make up. The bottom line of this philosophy is that it contributes to good leader and team development.

I use RFL every day. For instance, I am honored to be a member of the 2024 National Board of Directors of the Public Relations Society of America (PRSA). PRSA is the leading professional organization serving the communications community through a network of more than 400 professional and student chapters in the U.S., Argentina, Colombia, Peru, and Puerto Rico. I have been a PRSA member almost continuously since my time in the Air Force. The board position is my opportunity to apply RFL to the service of the organization's members. This is a great fit to lead ethically, advocating for members to make sure their voice is heard. I last made contributions representing members as a National Assembly Delegate-At-Large in 2011.

My PRSA memberships have included the National Capital, Hampton Roads, and Virginia Peninsula Chapters. This is my second opportunity to serve as a National Assembly Delegate-At-Large. I have also served the PRSA family as a Mid-Atlantic District Chair, a chapter president, and as the Hampton University (Virginia) PRSSA Chapter adviser for a few years.

My point here is that growing leadership and building teams relies on engagement. It is about getting people to connect, communicate, and collaborate. I hope you enjoy this new approach to training in a collaborative endeavor.

Acknowledgement

This project took shape when I was working with some amazing professionals on an educational video. Deirdre Breakenridge, Leslie Krohn, and James Goodwin were instrumental in helping me frame research and a conversation about trust and work location. Along the way, they helped me refocus my thoughts in leaders, members, and team development. I also want to thank Megan Breakenridge, graphic artist, for helping to shape and illustrate many of the thoughts contained in this work.

If you don't remember anything else that I tell you today, I would ask that you remember win-win collaborative culture that leads to shared understanding. Because you can talk about emotional intelligence, you can talk about empathy, you can talk about engagement, you can talk about organizational development, or you can talk about training, but they all rely on win-win situations for success. Whether win-win is achieved on purpose or by accident, a win-win collaborative culture with shared understanding makes the effort a little different than what you might be used to.

That's because there are so many times when it's just about the organization. What we've learned over the last few years about our world is that people got in touch with what they want. And sometimes that allows them to focus more on what they want and on what their life requires, and that may be different than what the organization requires. And I think we all know that this is not the traditional way that this all works. We're going to talk about that.

I need to build you a roadmap of how I approach this thing because I've studied it, and I've researched it, and I talk about it all the time. The roadmap gives you some tools, and then I'm going to give you a chance to practice improving your emotional intelligence. This way, I give you something you can take away from here and use in whatever way works for you.

For me, the bottom line of emotional intelligence is to understand your emotions, and the way you do things based on those emotions, and to understand the emotions of people around you and the way they do things based on those emotions. Then you try to find a balance, a collaboration, or a win-win situation. The key is that this win-win situation employs emotional intelligence for everyone who is involved. Once you start to understand those emotions, you can think about them and take some action.

I think some of you know someone who thinks they are a morning person, but they are not really a morning person. The person has not accepted it, but that person is not a morning person. And I'm sure you know a person who thinks they are funny, who says that "everybody thinks I'm funny." But they are not funny, and we all know it. So, we want everybody to get in touch with who they are and how they manage who they are, so we can have collaboration and engagement.

We're going to talk about the attributes of emotional intelligence. The way that I bring this to people is that I have developed *The Right Fit Leading (RFL) Process*. I use *The RFL Process* to teach and speak to you here. This process allows you to use emotional intelligence in the interactions that you are going to have with people.

Emotional intelligence can help you provide for needs: engagement needs, communication needs, and shared understanding.

Let me offer an uncomplicated way to remember the categories as you decide what you are going to do as you employ emotional intelligence. To achieve social awareness, you LISTEN. You are trying to make sense of where people are, and where you want them to be. You must do the same for yourself. You must understand that if you have decided that you don't want this job but you're going to stay in it, you must understand that your decision creates emotions in you that are going to affect the people who work with or for you.

Think ORGANIZE to remember self-management because everyone must do this. You must figure out what you need to do and work with others to determine what the team needs. Thinking about ENGAGE or INTERACT for effective communication should be easy to do. COLLABORATE will help you focus on relationship management. I talked about Leader-Member Exchange (LMX) Theory, and I researched it, and I wrote about it. It's about getting in touch with people first as a one-on-one relationship and then growing relationships to other communications. And then self-awareness is always about the need to LOOK IN THE MIRROR at yourself before you try to fix or help others.

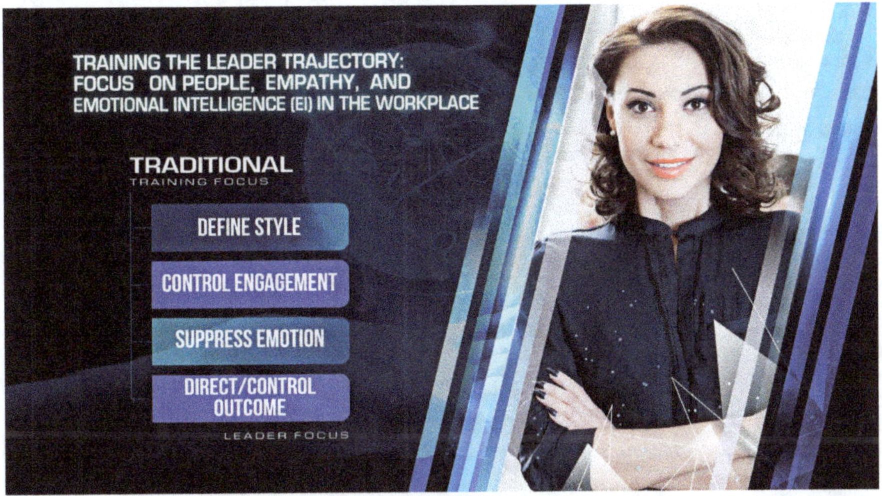

Figure 1: Training the Leader Trajectory

Here's the thing. Emotional intelligence can be simple if you can think about it in the way I talked about. Understand your emotions and the way you act on those emotions. And that could be as simple as, for me, if you don't let me have my first Diet Coke in the morning, we're going to have problems. I need that to get started. Just like some people need coffee.

Understand yourself and how you react. Understand others that you must interact with, and how they react to their emotions. Then try to find a middle ground. It might not be middle ground; it might be 60-40 in someone's favor to get it to work. But you must remember that the only way that you're going to understand their emotions and the way they react is to engage. Engagement is not just about talking to them after the meeting you scheduled. Engagement is not just about making them come into the office for one day so you can say you saw their face and you talked.

Engaging is an ongoing, questioning and answering relationship about what you need out of the job, and what I need out of the job, and how the job can provide for both of us that shared understanding. That's what we're really talking about. It is very important to fulfill these needs to address everyone's awareness.

But you really already have the help you need. You can analyze yourself. But you need to be open and honest and then you need to find ways to look at others. You need to listen, hear, understand, and synthesize before you take action.

One cannot develop leadership by only focusing on the leader and the skills needed to develop or improve. Using Leader-Member Exchange (LMX) Theory (Brown Sr., 2021), you can understand that leadership development is best done by developing and/or improving the skills of both the leader and those they lead. This approach leads to shared understanding that allows effective team building. This is the challenge that is addressed in this work. We are creating Motivationally Intelligent Teams.

Figure 2: Motivationally Intelligent Teams.

Motivationally Intelligent Teams combine coaching and mentoring techniques for the best results. These teams feature partnerships that pursue team and individual goals with equal importance. Team goals must come first, of course, but leaders of these teams recognize the need to find a balance with individual goals. Coaching involves asking open questions, enabling self-discovery, dispelling false feelings and beliefs, addressing changing situations, and looking to the future. Mentoring is about answering direct questions, providing information sources, seeking alternative answers, providing structure when needed, and considering the relevance of past experiences.

My conversations with leaders often indicate a need to change the focus of training from the traditional leader-centric philosophy to one of engagement, interaction, and collaboration. This creates an atmosphere where leaders and those they lead have equal opportunities to affect the leader-follower relationship that is required in effective teams.

Since 2021, I have taken a closer look at leadership training for various education and business projects. My analysis suggests that a lot of training courses, regardless of type (i.e., prescriptive, elective, etc.) are rooted in an authoritative approach. This approach suggests that the predominance of leadership styles expected and/or taught are dictated and driven by the leader/supervisor. Likewise, these styles are steeped in the expectation that the leader/supervisor can define his/her level of feedback, with little to no emotional investment involved with subordinates. In addition, this approach suggests that the success of the leader/supervisor/follower relationship is the lone responsibility of the "boss."

Some might say this way of thinking has some flaws, and even that this style of training misses the mark. Some might even say that those flaws can limit maximizing the interactive engagement in an effective leader/supervisor/follower relationship. In reality, what is perpetuated is a "disengaged" relationship in the work environment, a lack of understanding within teams, and poor collaboration toward meeting a desired end state.

My research addressed these issues, eventually leading me to create a brief on *"Training the Leader Trajectory: Focusing on People, Empathy, and Emotional Intelligence (EI) in the Workplace."* The brief focuses on an equitable work culture where all members, regardless of their role, have equal participation and decision-making ability in the operations and culture of the organization. This ensures that EI and empathy are inherent to the leadership style. Then, feedback is encouraged and expected of all parties. In turn, all parties can become emotionally invested in their efforts, and everyone is involved in attempts to achieve greater collaboration and teamwork.

"Training" analyzes the traditional leader-centric and employee-centric training methods, which are normally done separately. This brief's overall suggestion, consistent with the purpose of the book you are reading, is to train collaboratively for the best benefits. Leader-centric training is about defining styles and urging the leader to control engagement, suppress emotions, and direct or control the outcome. Employee-centric training prepares people to adjust to the leader's style by demonstrating how their input is considered during engagements and how their emotions are evaluated, or maybe how they are ignored, by those who lead them. Some current training allows collaboration where all inputs are considered to achieve outcomes. The limitation of this approach is that the leader may not get reporting from the training. They may get an after-action report later as a condition of the employee's attendance, but that does not necessarily lead to the kind of interactive communication required to retain what was learned or shared.

"Training" urges companies and leaders to be innovative and move to a collaborative, engaged approach to training. It suggests training teams together to create great relationships that can work on methods and trust while the training is in progress. The outcome should be shared understanding. This approach teaches everyone how to create collaborative relationships that can result in win-win relationships. In this way, the leader's style can connect emotions and empathy and all parties can share in open and honest deliberations. The collaborative effort affords all parties equal ability to provide feedback. If buy-in is achieved, all parties can accept responsibility for the desired outcomes.

Unfortunately, this approach was never formally presented to an organization. I was in a Senior Leader Development Program (SLDP) training as a Navy civilian at the time. However, I left civil service before having a chance to present a final project and complete the course. So, I share "Training" here as the precursor to *The RFL Process.*

The RFL Process is based on collaborative leadership. Collaborative Leadership has changed since its inception in the 1990s. It is deemed non-traditional when one considers that today's leadership tends to focus on power over people and the predominant needs of the organization. The change created by COVID-19 and other world pressures has led people to demand equal footing in how their work life is determined. People want win-win situations where their needs could have as much importance as that of the organization and/or the leader. It is a new search for equality in the workplace.

In the early 20th century, social worker Mary Parker Follett believed in the power of people working together, arguing that we need to form community to get things done (De Meyer, 2011, pp. 35-40). Follett talked about a creative process that is effective because the issues at hand are constantly reframed to make sense. So, we can conclude that "effective leadership requires collaboration, listening, influencing, and flexible adaptation, rather than command and control," according to Arnoud De

Meyer (2011, p. 36). He discusses the need for businesses to realize that the history of business leaders being held up as role models is being replaced by an increasingly skeptical society.

By training leaders and those they lead together, *The RFL Process* allows skill development in philosophy, inspiration, and motivation. It focuses on collaborative ways to create effective relationships and effective teams. Using EI and empathy, leaders get in touch with those they lead, seeking to master their own emotions and those of others. This approach is called engagement and it fosters the pursuit of win-win situations that are characterized by shared understanding. In addition, organizational development is improved as trust is developed and as cultural developments are observed.

Figure 3: Collaborative approach to training.

"Training" was a great start, but as I worked through this lens, *The RFL Process* emerged. The process characterizes leader and team development in terms of three key components: philosophy, inspiration, and motivation. Good leadership and follower-ship are tied to each other, whether they are taught and trained that way or not. My research supports the belief that *The RFL Process* promotes the creation of effective teams because it is based on EI and empathy for all members of any team, regardless of their position or level of responsibility.

The RFL Process addresses a consistent *philosophy* of how we lead and follow. It suggests that we must *inspire* ourselves and others. It also demonstrates the need to *motivate* ourselves and others to take on challenges that we might not attempt otherwise.

Figure 4: RFL overview

The RFL Process is effective for leader and team development. It starts with three major parts: 3D Philosophy, RAMP Inspiration, and CLUE Motivation. Each will be explained in depth in the chapters to come.

Next, the process helps us identify helpful tools for our training endeavors. We use EI and empathy, engagement, and LMX Theory to facilitate training. We also apply knowledge about the meaning of trust and how it is developed and nurtured. At this point, organizational development can turn its focus to what is needed for each leader and member. We use the principle of engaged interaction to help development subjects arrive at a shared understanding. LMX Theory and Engaged Interaction will be discussed in detail in Chapter 3.

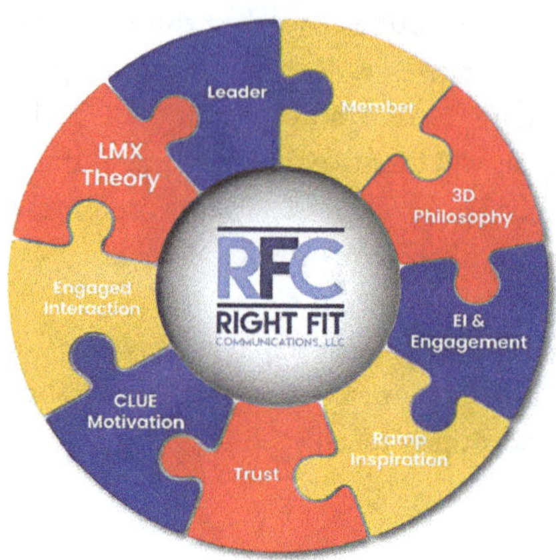

Figure 5: This is a formula for organizational and leadership development success.

This discussion of leader and member improvement based on EI will address the critical emphasis on philosophy, inspiration, and motivation. The discussion of philosophy is based on each person's approach and beliefs in this area. The discussion of inspiration and motivation will lead readers to develop and/or refine their own approaches.

The widespread use of EI in organizational development and training applications demonstrates the importance of collaborative decision-making. The abundance of online interactions continues to require that organizations find beneficial outcomes where leaders act in a prosocial manner. A prosocial attitude requires that the leader prioritize win-win situations whenever possible, seeking outcomes that are beneficial to all parties involved. It requires achieving buy-in through shared value, shared understanding, and good management of emotions. Prosocial behavior can be achieved with the EI, empathy, and engagement skills that are being developed in this work. With EI, we connect our own emotions with those of others to create collaboration in leadership communication, as shown in the illustration below.

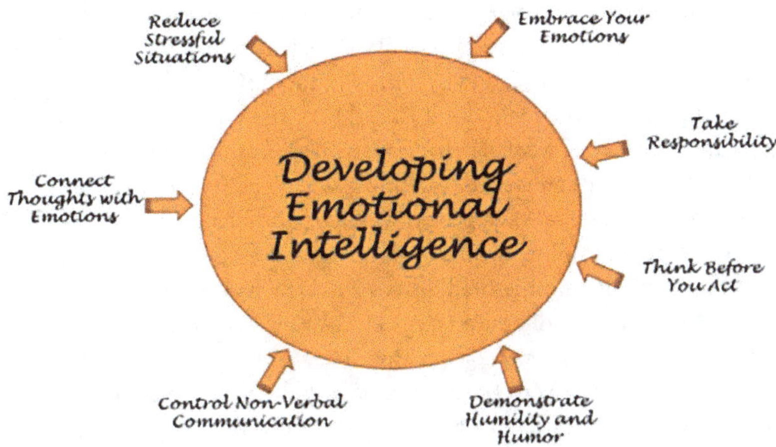

Figure 6: Developing EI.

Empathy requires that we understand another person's emotions, feeling them as if they are our own. Then we can act in support or mitigation. Problems can arise when people are forced into face-to-face interactions without the possibility of feedback and with no agreement on how to achieve shared understanding. This hinders collaborative communication.

It is important to engage with team members on a regular basis, and that engagement should be individual as often as possible. A common misunderstanding is about whether and how much engagement is involved. A 2012 study concerning engagement (Stillman) illustrates the great disagreement in the way leaders and their employees view engagement. In this study, CEOs, employees, and human resources professionals each answered questions about how they view their company in terms of engagement. The answers are very different in each group.

More than half of the CEOs surveyed believe that spontaneous feedback, or engagement, happens frequently in their organization. Also, more than 60 percent of employees cited a preference for immediate feedback, or engagement. However, less than 25 percent of employees said it is something they receive. Additionally, just 11 percent of the human resources people surveyed believed that employees receive immediate feedback. Finally, leaders, employees, and human resources professionals differed greatly on the existence of and frequency of recognition.

Because these three groups view feedback differently, we must examine our understanding of engagement. Yes, engagement is a powerful tool. Engagement requires communicating to achieve shared understanding. Engagement can also suggest policy or procedure adjustments once we identify an issue. The goal for leaders is that they practice and pursue engagement to achieve that shared understanding.

Here's an instance where engagement is important. An article I read highlighted a leader who uses a 3Cs rule. He said his results drive his decisions, his confidence leads to conviction in his approach, and he clearly communicates his direction and vision. Those are all great characteristics for a leader, but where is the mention of how he engages with people to get feedback that leads to shared understanding?

Similarly, I was at a conference in April 2023, participating in problem-solving groups. In one group, there was a person who had a problem with a new technology or app that was going to allow them to sign up for a program. But when they tried it, they could not submit, and the deadline passed. They had no ability to get the help they needed before the deadline. As the group I was in started to deliberate on what to do, they forgot the people part of the issue. They immediately set out to determine what went wrong, who was to blame, and how they could explain it to the bosses. They had to be reminded that issue #1 is fixing the problem for the person. The blame and the reasons will be part of that activity, but they should not be the most important consideration up front.

This is critical for leaders to understand. Leaders are responsible for people, and they should engage with those people to get things done. The success of those engagements can build trust, shared understanding, motivation, loyalty, performance, and accountability.

You can be successful with any leadership style. There may be challenges or obstacles along the way, but people very often find a way to survive and even prosper. Where they cannot, they often move on to another career. All of this is important because leadership is an action. Leadership is not about what you say, it is about what you do. The key to leadership is whether what you do resonates with those you lead.

If you are emotionally intelligent, empathic, engaging, and collaborative, it should be evident in your actions. This is just as important as what you say. If you listen intently and adjust to the feedback you receive, it will influence and motivate actions that matter. What I'm talking about is sharing your skills and your passion with those you lead. Seek out win-win relationships that strive for shared understanding and, when you don't have it, stop and work on it.

Leadership is a state of mind that you should share with your team. The team is watching you, and the team will follow you if your actions are worthy of it. More important, they will be your partners in achieving mission accomplishment.

This work focuses on training and development leaders and those they lead **AT THE SAME TIME!** A collaborative process is recommended as the best way to create and nurture successful teams. The chapters are geared to take you through a process that culminates in the collaborative training and team building that is recommended. This is all grounded in The RFL Process focusing on the 3D philosophy, EI, and empathetic endeavors.

This is how the chapters move you through the process and its benefits. *The RFL Process: A Deep Dive* teaches the process and all the ways it can be used. *Engagement and Training* takes a deeper dive to design and deliver training. *Theoretical Pathways* speaks to how the theoretical basis informs this journey. *Understanding Team Dynamics* and *Developing Motivationally Intelligent Teams* are geared to identify the teams needs and to understand how to create great interactions that lead to effective training and team building. *A Primer in Leadership Styles* is offered to demonstrate how leaders and those they lead can come together in collaborative interactions. *How Do We Teach It?* is a recommendation on how to teach The RFL Process and put it in practice to lead you to success. Also, there is a theory box at the end of several chapters to give you more resources in examining the issues in that chapter.

Now, we are ready to learn **The RFL Process**.

The RFL Process: A Deep Dive

Figure 7: A process for leader and team collaborative development.

As you learn ***The RFL Process***, you need a frame of reference. The process is focused on building leaders and teams. Now, let's examine the parts of ***The RFL Process***. Let me share my three primary, powerful tools that are available to communicate and develop teams effectively, building trust and holding everyone accountable.

- **3D = Philosophy**
- **RAMP = Inspiration**
- **CLUE = Motivation**

I use my leadership philosophy, **3D**, to be effective using these and other tools. **3D** is ***Dedication, Detail, Discipline***. We must be **dedicated**, committing to prepare and perform while motivating every step of the way. We must pay attention to **detail**, creating shared understanding to enhance strengths and improve weaknesses. We must be **disciplined**, following rules to be the best we can in every situation we face.

The bottom line is to know yourself and your team and to develop together to form a winning combination that can withstand the test of time. Work together through the common language of **3D** and through a shared understanding.

3D Philosophy

Figure 8: 3D leadership philosophy.

My leadership philosophy is captured in my book 3D Coaching: Suggestions for a New Approach (Brown, 2021). I refined it during my time in the military and as a sports coach. Let us examine the philosophy closely. First, there are key questions we can ask ourselves, illustrated in the graphic below.

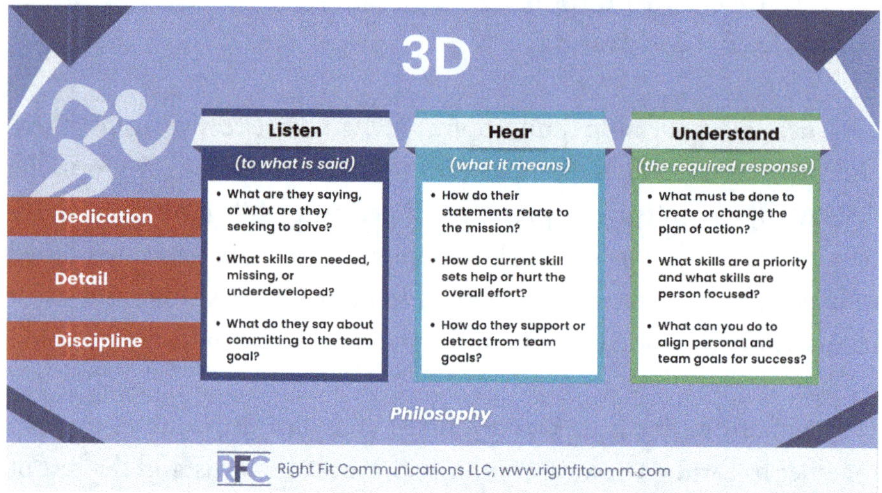

Figure 9: Your team agrees to commit to be dedicated, focus on vital details, and honor discipline in all things.

Dedication

Dedication is about what we believe. We must look inside ourselves and determine our fundamental beliefs about life and love and faith. This is important because our lives are guided by those concepts even if we are not aware of it. Dedicating ourselves to something that goes against those values can put us in a difficult pursuit of purpose and contentment. This is key for the team dynamic.

A good fit between person and organizational values is important to our success. Values help us work through the challenges we face every day. If your values match those of your leader or team, it can be easier to make decisions and contribute to team goals and objectives. There may still be struggles, but finding a good fit in this way can lead to effective collaboration.

Stress can come into play if there is a disconnect between your personal values and the leader. Leaders may have difficulty with this kind of conflict because it can create a struggle to do the things the organization needs in terms of organization versus personal values.

Sometimes, conflict can be beneficial, such as when there is a new leader or there is a major change in the team. The resulting adjustment period might be a healthy transition experience if leaders can align their values sufficiently once they understand the team values.

Achieving a "good fit" is challenging because changes in leaders and members and administrative aspects of the organization present a challenge in finding an acceptable balance between personal and team values. In the end, *Dedication* requires commitment to giving heart and soul in pursuit of achieving and maintaining balance between person and organization.

Detail

Detail is the work "where the rubber meets the road." Honing your skills requires being open to learning new things and to developing current skills to another level. It requires striving to improve on today's performance, even if today featured you winning an organizational award for your achievements. Success is a never-ending journey. One who is content just to enjoy yesterday's accomplishment may not be capable of achieving the focus and effort that will be required in the future. Your accomplishments may raise your or the organization's expectations going forward. Attention to detail and hard work are the things that keep you achieving at a good rate, or that at least keep you striving for improvement.

Strive for accuracy in all things and, as you succeed, you might experience risks. These risks could include failing to manage the day's events and being late for work, missing deadlines, or even failing to follow proper work procedures. Understand that there are risks in your organization and work to identify, analyze, and quantify them so you can work to eliminate or to mitigate them.

Work towards a state of perfection by identifying the tasks needed to succeed and carefully working through them. Use repetition to make task accomplishment a habit. *Detail* requires diligence and communication through effective listening skills. Take all the time that is required to achieve the desired outcomes. Understand that preparation, planning, and design are the keys to setting up clearly defined processes that move you and your team toward improved performance.

Listen to your team members about what they are experiencing as they learn and perfect their skills. Allow everyone the opportunity to question what is going on and to suggest ways they want to approach things that are difficult for them. By listening, you may be surprised at how much team members appreciate your attention. Listening allows you to get more information about issues people are struggling with, examine new approaches that might not have been considered, or identify a potential threat to success. These possibilities are directly linked to the way you can build trust through open communication. Now, you are building or nurturing a culture where people feel comfortable sharing information about problems when they are first discovered.

Discipline

It is important to deal with preventative, supportive, and corrective *Discipline* to help with person and team development. Use preventative discipline to identify desired behaviors and create awareness. Use supportive discipline to redirect or reshape undesirable actions. Use corrective discipline to eliminate or mitigate undesired behaviors. Examine your team or training task and focus on the behaviors that are considered most favorable to meet your objectives.

As we discuss *Dedication* and *Detail*, we suggest methods that should guide organization-friendly actions in the process of addressing

Discipline. This is a way to limit or eliminate undesirable behaviors and make corrective discipline unnecessary.

The chart below should be helpful in keeping 3D concepts available as your team communicates and operates together.

Dedication	*Detail*	*Discipline*
ded·i·ca·tion /dedə'kāSH(ə)n/: *Noun*: the quality of being dedicated or committed to a task or purpose.	**de·tail** /də'tāl, /'dētāl/ *Noun*: an individual feature, fact, or item.	**dis·ci·pline** /'disəplən/ *Noun*: to train or develop by instruction and exercise, especially in self-control.
Leadership Note: Success has a price. That price is dedication to the task at hand through hard work. That price is being determined to do the best you can, win or lose. That price is applying the best of yourself to everything you do.	*Leadership Note: Paying attention to detail means demonstrating to your team, and yourself, that it is necessary to focus on the journey, not just today's goal. Learning the right way to work and be productive is vital to having the confidence to grow as a person and as a team member. The leader's job is to create the perfect conditions for success by teaching techniques and strategy. Once that is accomplished your team can use their talents and their wits to grow and win.*	*Leadership Note: Discipline is important all the time, but it takes on more importance when things go wrong. You cannot change what happens, but your discipline provides you with the tools to change your approach, your attitude, and/or your response. Discipline guides your ability to avoid complaining in troubled times and instead working with your team to figure out how to make things better.*

Figure 10: 3D principles.

The way ***Discipline*** is defined in 3D is supportive. Discipline moves leaders and members to work together to discover individual potential and move everyone toward continued success. There are many ways we can be supportive. For instance, leaders can change strategies or techniques to be sure they are capturing the attention and motivation of all members of the team.

Organizations can also be supportive by showing interest in each person's life beyond the current situation by asking questions and making comments to foster good communication. Always use eye contact to demonstrate genuine interest in the person. When someone is struggling with a skill, use physical proximity to demonstrate commitment to their improvement and to get them back on track.

One can also resort to suggesting other ways to do a task when there is an issue or problem. One can be provided with small, incremental challenges as another way to help find ways to manage the work on their own. For instance, ask the person if they would like to continue working to master the current skill with the group, or whether they would like to have private instruction at another time. These kinds of approaches take the spotlight off the person's struggle, at least for the moment.

Supportive *Discipline* focuses on what works best for each person and provides ways for them to pursue the best approach. While this kind of discipline may cause disconnects in the team, they should be short-lived, and the team may be stronger when the person in question fixes the problem and rejoins the group effort.

RAMP Inspiration

Figure 11: Formula to inspire training outcomes.

Leaders can find success by managing the job competence, networking needs, personal growth, and life concerns of themselves and those they lead. My RAMP approach can help.

Relate: Start with relating to those you are responsible for; engage with them. Let us talk about engagement. There is a common misunderstanding about whether engagement is necessary and about how much time it deserves. A 2012 study concerning engagement (Stillman, 2012) illustrates the great disagreement in the way leaders and their employees view engagement. In this study, CEOs, employees, and human resources professionals each answered questions about how they view their company in terms of engagement. The answers are very different in each group.

More than half of the CEOs surveyed believe that spontaneous feedback, or engagement, happens frequently in their organization. Also, more than 60 percent of employees cited a preference for immediate feedback, or engagement. However, less than 25 percent said it is something they receive. Additionally, just 11 percent of the human resources people surveyed believed that employees receive immediate feedback. Finally, leaders, employees, and human resources professionals differed greatly on the existence of and frequency of recognition.

Because these three groups view feedback differently, we must reconsider our understanding of engagement. Yes, engagement is a powerful tool. Engagement requires communicating to get everyone on the same page at the same time. Engagement can also suggest policy or procedure adjustments once we identify an issue. The goal for leaders is that they practice and pursue engagement to achieve that shared understanding.

To get it right, make sure that you are a contributing member of the team. It is easy to say, "I would not ask you to do anything I would not do." But you must do "it" at least once.

Anticipate: Look beyond today. Analyze the work that is going on and try to understand what comes next. Get in touch with forward-thinking members of your team to discuss possible courses of action beyond the tasks that are just being completed on time. Can you get ahead? You do not have to be a visionary, but at least think through what might come next.

As you tackle today's work and tomorrow's possibilities, keep in touch with the team's wellbeing. Find out what the team needs and make sure it gets provided or satisfied. Remember that you cannot assign every job to a superstar, so there will be times when a role player or substitute must bring the project to completion. Stay connected to what needs to be done and do not let anything fall through the cracks. See the work required, then delegate, persuade, direct, or do it yourself.

Motivate: Set very high goals. Easy to reach goals do not get the adrenaline pumping. Set the bar of success high enough to make people sweat.

For instance, sometimes the work does not get done. Often, companies and their leaders get anxious when deciding on having "the talk" with employees, but remember that "the talk" can be positive or negative. So there is no need to avoid it. Make needed corrections or reassignments. These activities tend to be less stressful if leaders have created trusting relationships with those they lead. Leaders must employ open and honest communication at every opportunity.

Participate: Do not let anyone work harder than you do. Set the example and keep the team ready for action. A leader who works hard often puts pressure on the team to keep up.

Most of all, engage and collaborate with others. Leaders who try to do it all themselves often fail. Leaders who believe they are solely responsible for success and failure often end up in stressful situations. Since we know that no one has all the answers, we can say that getting more people involved in meaningful decision-making offers more resources in getting the job done. You have opportunities to hear different points of view or innovative thinking.

Make sure your actions in communicating are good for all involved. You might have to sacrifice your own wants and desires at times to allow other interests to prevail for the good of the communication effort. Be fair in your actions and make sure the process is fair. Try to focus on a win-win outcome wherever possible and be prepared to compromise when that is not possible.

CLUE Motivation

CLUE is a helpful formula for developing or refining leadership skills. There are 4 ways leaders can ensure successful communications.

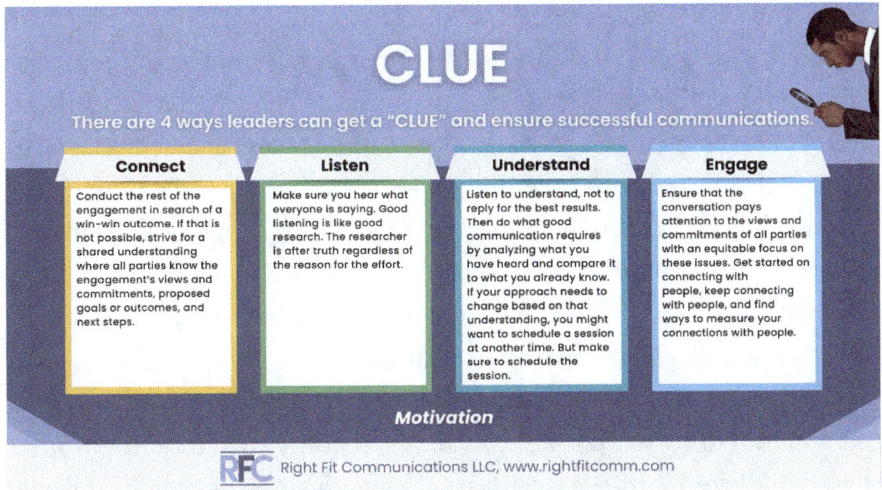

Figure 12: Method for successful communications.

Connect: Conduct the rest of the engagement in search of a win-win outcome. If that is not possible, strive for a common purpose or outcome. Make sure that all parties know the engagement's views and commitments, proposed goals or outcomes, and next steps.

Listen: Make sure you hear what everyone is saying. Good listening is like good research. The researcher is after truth regardless of the reason for the effort.

Understand: Listen to understand, not to reply for the best results. Then do what good communication requires by analyzing what you have heard and comparing it to what you already know. If your approach needs to change based on that understanding, you might want to schedule a session at another time. *But make sure to schedule the session.*

Engage: Ensure that the conversation pays attention to the views and commitments of all parties with an equitable focus on these issues. Get started on connecting with people, keep connecting with people, and find ways to measure the effectiveness of your connections with people.

So, **CLUE** leads us to creating and nurturing relationships as an effective way to motivate people. It is not always easy to motivate because, to be good at it, one must pay attention and take the necessary actions as the organizational environment evolves. That evolution affects people and work relationships, and good engagement can help you stay connected with how things are progressing. Motivational goals can be addressed through mutual understanding. This understanding contributes to cohesion in work relationships and dynamic change. Motivation and leadership development should be team activities that, when done well, create great relationships.

Motivation tends to be situational, and the pursuit of it often seems to come down to whose interests have the most weight, and who has the telling "voice" in the decision-making effort (Roberts & O'Reilly III, 1973). Voice is that part of the deliberations that carries the most weight when the final decisions are made. Remember, our examination of training is focused on giving everyone a voice to learn and to grow.

There are three pillars that define motivation in the workplace: choice, effort, and persistence (Latham, 2012). Further, motivation is an integral aspect of training and is a core competency of leadership. Galvanizing and inspiring people to exert effort are key requirements for effective leadership. Getting people to give committed, persistent effort in the pursuit of an organization's values or goals is what motivation is all about.

C.A. O'Reilly (1991) found that the majority of organizational behavior studies focus on goal setting and equity theories. That means that organizational justice principles are as much about leadership as they are about employee motivation. There are two things to consider: (1) Distributive justice focuses on what was distributed, who it was distributed to, and who received what distribution; and (2) Procedural justice is concerned with whether there are procedures, processes, or systems in place for determining what was distributed to whom.

We can look to the work of Gary P. Latham, who discussed key factors that affect feelings of procedural justice as a priori criteria for making decisions and "voice" (Latham, 2012). When consistently applied, the a priori criteria tend to suppress bias, allowing actions to be based on accurate information, as well as on other logical considerations. Latham believed that people are likely to accept and understand the basis for an organizational decision even when they do not necessarily agree with it. Voice is the concept of participation in decision making. In other words, people may be willing to support decisions that are not congruent with their earlier viewpoint if the situation allows them to feel that their voice will be heard and will carry some weight with the leader or organization.

The widespread applicability of principles of organizational justice to the workplace is a clear reason for using it as a tool in our training endeavors. Now, we can discuss the importance of engagement.

The RFL process has some foundation in the writings of T.A. Ryan and P.C. Smith (1954), who argued for new paradigms of experimental and clinical psychology. They argued that it was useless and misleading to try to translate worker goals into the 1925 argument of watson concerning stimuli and responses. The difficulty, they argued, was that Watson's assertion implies that the laws that govern these stimuli and responses in experimental laboratory paradigms are the same as those that hold for all other stimuli and responses in everyday situations. They argued, instead, for a focus on the wants, wishes, desires, and experiences of the individual.

Engagement and Training

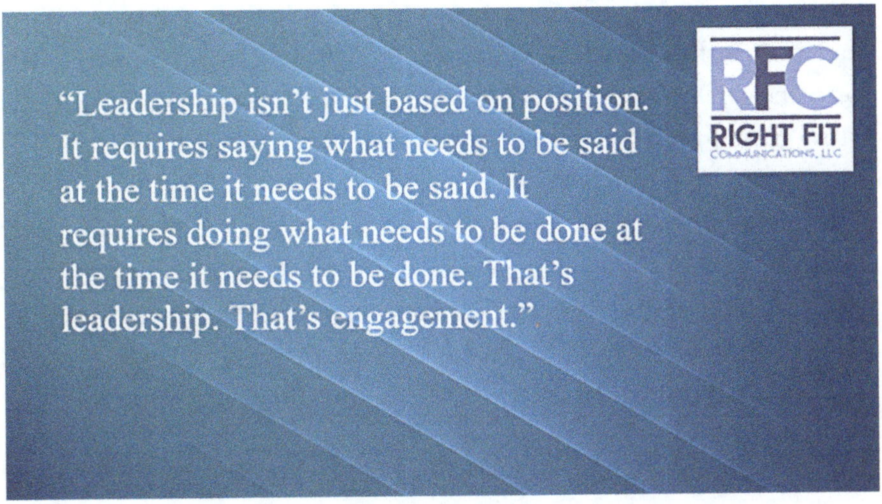

"Leadership isn't just based on position. It requires saying what needs to be said at the time it needs to be said. It requires doing what needs to be done at the time it needs to be done. That's leadership. That's engagement."

RFC
RIGHT FIT
COMMUNICATIONS, LLC

Figure 13: Dr. Brown on leadership.

Engagement is valuable. It helps leaders connect with their team to achieve shared understanding. Engagement can also suggest policy or procedure adjustments once issues are identified. The goal for leaders is that they practice and pursue engagement to achieve that shared understanding.

Leaders who fail to engage with their team members on a regular basis can put them in difficult, unfortunate situations. Leaders who only engage with team members when there is a deadline may find themselves in difficult conversations. The leader who does not take the time to regularly engage with their people and get to know them is taking a risk.

A leader may identify someone's strengths and weaknesses, but do they know what brings people to work each day? Does the leader know which tasks people enjoy most? Does the leader have tasks in mind that would offer people new job challenges? Does the leader know where people want to be personally and professionally next week, next month, or next year?

Engagement helps leaders find answers and create relationships. Leaders must be patient when managing because changes probably will not come fast or easy. Persistence and cooperation should bring long-lasting trust and communication that will make any organization more effective and more fun to be a part of.

Leaders have a great opportunity to inspire people by being calm when there is chaos, by being deliberate when there is doubt, and by caring when there is trouble. They can make sure every person enjoys the journey by striving to be the kind of emotionally intelligent leader we are training in these pages, and by connecting with those who do the same.

I am reminded of an article called *"How to Spot an Incompetent Leader."* It focused in part on the importance of a leader taking a personal assessment to determine their effectiveness. The article suggests that one of the ways to judge a leader's effectiveness is by combining a personal assessment with an assessment from those you lead. It is important to find out what they want, what they like, what makes them tick, and to incorporate that into the way you lead them. Sometimes you can't find a fit, but that too is a growth opportunity.

I used to have a running joke with someone who worked for me. I would always say, "I get you," to let that person know that I'm listening and that I'm trying to maintain our connection of sharing responsibility and accountability. This might be helpful for you in some future situations. The leader who does not take the time to regularly engage with their people to get to know them is taking a risk.

Leaders must engage with their staffs in any way they can. Also, all involved parties need to see quality results from this engagement. My research takes a straightforward approach about leading people, focusing on three areas: engagement, role-setting, and personal growth.

It's simple. But it takes discipline to master. Focus on engaging by setting roles that all understand and by developing members through communication. Be empathetic and make the connection with people who will be the keys to your success.

Figure 14: Engagement is a key to success.

Know yourself and your team and develop together to form a winning combination that can withstand the test of time. Work together through the common language of *3D* to make sure everyone is on the same page and heading in the same direction. Find ways to ensure that all members want to work toward a common outcome.

This approach helps leaders create strong relationships, bond with their people, and inspire others. Focusing on people can also result in achieving collaborative, communicative relationships where trust is built and nurtured. The resulting improvements can deliver increased personal and professional growth, improved productivity and performance, and innovation.

Trust and collaboration can improve engagement efforts. In fact, much research has addressed trust in the workplace.

Overview on Trust

Latham discussed four beliefs in work motivation that we should keep in mind as we train and develop people. They are (1) money as a motivator, (2) the distinction between intrinsic and extrinsic motivators, (3) the causal relationship between job satisfaction and job performance or the converse, and (4) the importance of participation in decision making as a motivational technique.

As we work toward training effectiveness, we look to Latham to strengthen our skill development and goal setting activities (Latham & Budworth, 2007). We can also agree with Robert and Joyce Hogan in terms of Socioanalytic Theory (2001). The theory asserts that people are constantly in need of either getting along or getting ahead. They are pursuing "getting along" when they pursue acceptance, approval, and popularity. They are pursuing "getting ahead" when they focus their efforts on the need for power, control, and status. Interpersonal relationships are inherently problematic because of the dichotomy of actions. One can solve the problem of getting along by simply acting in a way that would avoid disapproval. However, to get ahead one may need to adopt more active and manipulative forms of self-presentation.

Figure 15: Socioanalytic Theory.

Whether one is trying to get along or get ahead, trust is important in every organization and every leader should be actively building trust. This is done through continuous engagement in a collaborative relationship that allows trust to develop. Leaders can nurture that development by instilling in every member an understanding of their value to the group. Building trust in this way can contribute to achieving organizational goals and to encouraging cooperation from all members.

Every organization needs trust. Every leader needs to be continuously engaged in building and maintaining trust within their team. The leader's emphasis should always be on the individual as a performing and valuable part of the group. Work hard to involve every person when dealing with the group. Make comments all-inclusive at every opportunity. This builds trust, fosters belonging, and reduces the noise in the channel. Noise is a distraction in communication. The significance of noise here is that the more times you deliver a message, the more chance there is that it might change from its original meaning. An all-inclusive delivery promotes a "one goal, one voice" approach to communicating.

The way to ensure the message is delivered efficiently is to create a communication zone that provides the best environment for interaction. A communication zone is the place where social bonding takes place to create close ties and exchange feedback. Participants in the communication zone agree to a "contract" of paying attention and responding to messages (Nardi & Whittaker, 2002). The "zone" is typically a physical environment that allows participants to understand each other's state of work in an attempt to find common reference points and common orientations (Leinonen, Järvelä, & Häkkinen, 2005, pp. , p 303). The communication zone can be created virtually, but face-to-face meetings tend to be much more powerful and interactive for this purpose.

Exchanging feedback and agreeing to the "contractual" sharing of information can be considered a two-pronged approach to communication zones. The value of the face-to-face interaction cannot be ignored, according to two researchers who argue that there is a rich body of research listing this as the most information-rich medium (Nardi & Whittaker, 2002, pp., p 84-86). Relationships grow and trust develops when the parties exchange expressions of commitment to communication. Now teams can create an environment where members interact freely regardless of the message and where feedback is the norm and not the exception.

What is social bonding? It is engaging sender and receiver in social interaction and using informal conversation. Effective social bonding is about awareness and having a sense of the other person's "presence," which includes their physical appearance, body language, and facial expressions. Skilled communicators will also have a sense of the other person's makeup, jewelry, hair style, and clothing, because they all say something about the person. Additional benefits come from off-the-cuff conversation such as family questions, gossip, jokes, or just idle chat. Social bonding is an invaluable way to empower all communication participants.

Once in the communication zone, participants adjust to barriers to communication. We will focus on part of a list provided by the Agency for Healthcare Research and Quality (O'Daniel & Rosenstein, 2008). The barriers of concern are:

- Personal values and expectations.
- Personality differences.
- Hierarchy.
- Disruptive behavior.

- Differences in language and jargon.
- Fears of diluted professional identity.
- Differences in accountability and rewards; and
- Emphasis on rapid decision making.

Personal values and expectations can cause problems in communication. This is because each person can get wrapped up in their own point of view. Common ground is the key to overcoming this barrier. If each party can work to understand the other's point of view, they can work toward adjustments that make message delivery and receipt easier. Shared understanding can also help to ensure that no person's values are negatively affected by the interaction.

Taking special care not to create or escalate an emotionally charged topic can help us overcome personality differences. That's because people might see things differently based on their personality and other factors. Sometimes, it is best to avoid topics that create an uncomfortable atmosphere. If an emotionally charged topic must be discussed, ensure that you have an agreement on the shared expectations by all parties and that the session can be stopped or rescheduled should problems occur.

Another barrier has to do with hierarchy, and you can overcome it by increasing and improving daily communication between upper and lower levels of the organization. You can also ensure that each person's skills and knowledge are valued, and that each voice is heard whenever possible. In one-on-one situations that require a participative decision, try to meet somewhere other than in the higher-ranking person's office. A neutral place, like a break room or a coffee shop, can be a great choice.

When dealing with disruptive behavior, be deliberate in your approach and professional in your actions. Let the other person know up front that the behavior will not be tolerated. Don't continue the communication until the other person commits to the change in behavior and stop the communication if the person reverts to the disruptive behavior. Be consistent with these actions whenever you deal with disruptive behavior.

A difference in language and jargon is an especially challenging barrier to communication. The best way to address this is to prepare in advance. Find out about your subject or subjects to determine whether this will be a problem. If the problem is a difference in language, schedule an interpreter. If the problem is one of semantics or dialect based on the cultural leanings of participants, it might help to agree on some terms of reference that will come up in the conversation. The way to address jargon is to make a conscious attempt to avoid it. When it creeps in, define what is really being discussed.

Fears of diluted professional identity are really about people worrying that something that is said or done in the communication will affect their standing or their career. The key here is open and honest communication that allows each participant equal standing in the interaction. A culture of professional courtesy is also helpful in putting people at ease.

When people are treated differently in terms of accountability and rewards, it hinders the communication process. Whether it's a one-on-one or multiple relationship interaction, every person must have the same accountability for the discussion and the outcome. At the same time, every person must have an equal opportunity to be rewarded and the reward process must be specific and transparent.

The final barrier is emphasis on rapid decision making. There is often no time to address other barriers when the decision must be made rapidly. The best approach is to let everyone know up front that there will be limited discussion before the final decision. If possible, inform the people or the group about why the decision must be made so rapidly. The key to success in terms of this barrier to communication is to have a professional, collaborative, trusting culture that will help everyone deal with what could be a difficult action. Setting up a person or a team in a collaborative agreement and then deciding without collaborating is risky, but this is sometimes a necessary action for a leader or an organization.

Barriers to communication are always a part of interactions in some way. The best way to ensure that they are being addressed is to have an organizational climate that is conducive to managing the issues. For instance, the organization should have a unifying philosophy of open and honest communication. Members should be committed to the common goal of collaboration and should be willing to share responsibilities. The organization must have an established process for negotiation of goals and roles as the work evolves. The organization should also have a process for resolving conflicts between team members. In addition, all team members should be aware of the organization's complaint or grievance process. All these actions prepare the team for the dynamics of organizational change.

Collaboration

Use collaboration when setting the "next" plan that will bring organizational success. Leaders are often excited to create their grand plan either when they find that "best new way" or when they take over a new job and set out to improve things. In both cases, leaders expect their team to be just as excited about this new plan as they are. The same leaders may find disappointment when their team does not respond positively to the plan.

If your people do not understand your plan because you have not adequately explained the purpose and procedures, they will probably be slow to jump for joy. More important, if the team has reservations and you have already set the new plan in motion, you may meet with strong emotions against this new initiative. You may encounter big problems if you do not socialize the plan with your team before implementing it.

I am not saying that the leader must get approval of the plan from subordinates and colleagues. I am not saying the leader must achieve buy-in before the plan can work. What I am saying is that collaboration as the plan is developed allows the change to be built in, not bolted on. When people are given the opportunity to build the plan along the way they are far more interested and motivated to see it through to success.

The collaborative approach works because it keeps everyone on the same page, and it identifies challenges along the way. This is about a team.

We see so many stories about getting away from bad bosses or choosing to be happy when things do not go well at work. These are certainly coping mechanisms; however, some of the situations we see put all the responsibility, and sometimes the blame, on the employee. The reason for this is sometimes that the employee is often the only one who is REQUIRED to change in a bad situation. I am sure you heard something like, "the leader has the deciding vote." While true, it can often make a bad situation worse.

So, I urge leaders to grade themselves every day using the eyes and viewpoint of their workforce. See what you are doing from their seat. If you cannot see it, ask them. Nevertheless, be prepared because you may not like what you hear. The interesting thing is that even if you do not ask them, they are telling you what is right and wrong if you will only listen.

When you grade yourself, ask the tough questions:

- Did I tell them their work is important?
- Did I clearly explain why I was not satisfied with the outcome?
- Did I make a review about the task or about the person? Did I consider both?
- Did I treat the person the way I want to be treated?
- Did I give them a chance to give their side of the story?
- Did I give them a chance to use their expertise?
- Was I clear about what I wanted at the beginning?

Asking these questions daily, or at least each time a major task is completed, can deliver two valuable things to your leadership journey. First, they will give a voice to those you lead. Second, they will remind you about what is important. Developing leaders is about creating and nurturing relationships.

People in leadership development courses are taught to control emotions, take responsibility, think before acting, control all types of communication, and reduce stressful situations. In terms of controlling emotions, it is important to clarify that EI focuses on embracing emotions. EI teaches us to take the appropriate action based on your emotions and the emotions of those around you.

What leadership development training sometimes misses is the cultivation of relationships. How many times has the boss gone off to training and come back with grand ideas for change while the workers ensured business as usual? How many times have workers gone off to training and had no opportunity to share what they learned? In both cases, the leadership development value can be lost when the course is over.

I am in favor of team training and role reversal where leaders and team members can bond and grow as a unit. One way to do this in training is to specify a task that must be completed and a report that must be done within strict time limits. The trick is to make a non-leader the boss and only give the details, the end state, and the reporting requirements to that person. The new boss then "trains" the team and accomplishes the task. Of course, there will be challenges and maybe even uncomfortable situations, but an experienced moderator can help the team through those times. This would of course be followed by an out brief led by the moderator.

Using this method, the team comes back from the training with a better understanding of each other. This understanding is important to building your cohesive unit that not only understands each other, but that has found a way to manage through the tough times.

Whether your organization uses this approach or some other one, I suggest you keep Communication Accommodation Theory as the foundation of your efforts to bond the team together. The theory shows you how to adjust verbal and nonverbal interactions while emphasizing or minimizing differences between participants. These interactions use language, context, identity, and intergroup and interpersonal factors to find common ground. With collaboration, leadership development depends on every member of the team.

What we have been discussing is that effective collaboration supports trusting relationships when it creates an environment that allows people to share work and understand each person's situation. It is also valuable when it creates open and honest group communications.

Leaders can be effective when they engage at all levels of the organization. This engagement ensures that each employee knows their value because they are included in a win-win collaboration that creates shared understanding. Trust is also strengthened when leaders and members share feedback, especially when someone is excluded from interactions for whatever reason.

This work uses behaviorism as a foundation for engagement and training efforts. B.F. Skinner (1966) asserted that changes in behavior are the result of an individual's response to events (stimuli) that occur in the environment. A response produces a consequence such as defining a word, hitting a ball, or solving a math problem. Skinner analyzed Stimulus-Response (S-R) patterns, arguing that when a particular S-R pattern is reinforced (rewarded), the individual is conditioned to respond. Reinforcement is the key, and a reinforcer is anything that strengthens the desired response.

3

Theoretical Pathways

This chapter discusses LMX Theory and Engaged Interaction in more detail. It also offers other theories or resources that will be helpful in leader and team development.

LMX Theory

Figure 16: LMX Theory focuses on two-way relationships.

LMX Theory helps leaders examine their leadership style in terms of individual relationships as opposed to dealing with entire groups as if every person were the same. It facilitates building great organizations that people will always want to be part of. Leaders who engage and bond with their people have an opportunity to be rewarded with superior performance, outstanding motivation, and loyalty. Every leader should make interacting with people their daily priority.

LMX Theory builds collaborative relationships that are geared to value personal goals and dignity. LMX can be effective in developing new teams or in building teams during a major change, for example. This focus on two-way collaborative communication fosters rapid evaluation of current skills and promotes a convenient way to segment people into groups for greatest efficiency.

LMX can align your team into two groups, each possessing similar skills and abilities. This gets people working and possibly avoids some of the team-forming tensions that may arise using other leadership techniques. LMX relationships between leaders and their subordinates go through three stages: role taking, role making, and routinization. Role taking happens when members first join the group. This is when members demonstrate their skills and abilities and when the leader forms first impressions. Role making is when the leader creates a role for the new member, or when the member may assume a certain role based on their capabilities. Routinization is about developing the practices the person or team will follow in pursuit of stated goals.

LMX is effective in these situations, but those who use the theory's in-group/out-group segmentation must avoid making that identification a permanent arrangement. One of the keys to this book's approach is the importance of collaboration, which need adaptability or flexibility to succeed. This is important to allow members who show progress an opportunity to join the group that is performing the best. Also, as leaders grow their people and build their teams, they should look at mixing the groups to increase capability and allow within-group mentoring.

Developing dyadic (two-way) relationships can drive leader effectiveness and indicate the best way to build groups. Measure the dyadic relationships in terms of the level of loyalty, support, respect, and trust among all parties. The quality of the relationships influence all of the business success factors – decision making, access to resources, responsibility, and member performance (Janse, 2019).

LMX is a powerful way to develop all members of your team and to find cohesion.

Engaged Interaction

The listen, hear, understand principle of engaged interaction is illustrated in the graphic below (Brown, 2017, pp., p. 148).

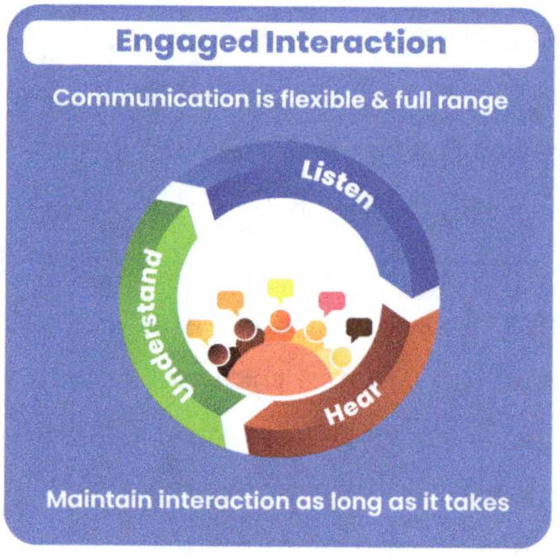

Figure 17: Engaged interaction is about full-range communications.

Leaders are always told about listening skills but not always about "hearing." What did the person really say? Leaders should strive for a comfortable learning environment that invites people to freely engage and provide feedback. It is important to minimize distractions by removing barriers to communication like the use of jargon, physical barriers, and differences in language or culture. To truly hear the other person, avoid multitasking, make eye contact, and ask questions for clarification so that information is truly shared in the communication. Always pay attention to feedback and, if you don't get any, ask more questions.

Engaged Interaction requires empathy to see what others see and to understand what they think about what they see. This effort is important, so if you can't understand, then ask more questions. Engaged Interaction connects with EI and empathy in three parts: knowing yourself, knowing others, and knowing the goal.

- Know Yourself: Engage in open and honest interactions by accepting your feelings.
- Know Others: Strive to understand their thoughts, feelings, and their commitment to the communication activity.
- Know the Goal: Once you understand yourself and others, you can tailor the communication to best suit everyone's needs.

Engaged interaction can be enhanced using strategic flexibility, which is the ability to act in response to external environmental changes, or to drive intentional changes and adapt to environmental changes. Strategic flexibility changes the message in response to internal and external influences to increase the chances that the message will achieve its desired result. This concept involves several steps (Brown, 2017, pp. , p. 154):

- Assess the situation.
- Evaluate the communication environment.
- Use various skills (tone of voice, gestures, expressions, body language, etc.).

- Be creative.
- Don't be afraid to adapt or change.
- Reassess and reevaluate.

Engaged Interaction requires that we must listen to what is being said, then take the time to hear the words and decipher them. Then, and only then, we should determine what action or response is needed considering the message received. Engaged Interaction is achieved when all parties participate in flexible, full-range communication. This open and flexible communication must continue until interaction and shared understanding are achieved.

LMX and Engaged Interaction help leaders and their teams develop strong relationships where they bond with and inspire each other. The resulting improvements in the work environment can deliver increased personal and professional growth, improved productivity and performance, and innovation. As we grow teams, it is important to examine performance versus productivity. Performance is based on output only, while productivity focuses on output in relation to input.

Figure 18: Productivity is a more effective measurement than performance.

Place your emphasis on productivity when training and building teams. Determine the level of mental and physical contribution that people are giving and take care of them. Understand their contribution, guide their contribution, or adjust their contribution to achieve success. Just remember that whatever is done should be done with engagement between people.

The training focus available through *The RFL Process* has EI and empathy as its foundation. Two additional theories are helpful for those who embrace EI. Sensemaking Theory is a collaborative process that creates shared awareness and understanding out of different individuals' perspectives and varied interests. Communication Accommodation Theory (CAT) addresses adjusting verbal and nonverbal interactions to emphasize or minimize differences between participants. These interactions use language, context, identity, and intergroup and interpersonal factors to find common ground.

Sensemaking Theory

Figure 19: Sensemaking Theory in practice.

Sensemaking is the social activity of decoding messages by drawing upon a common language and managing the actions in which we engage (Brown, 2017, pp. , p. 59). A social context of sharing ideas and influencing how others make sense of events is enhanced by creating trusting relationships.

Leaders apply this theory through connected communications and structured reinforcement. Connected communications are face-to-face, routine discussions with your team members dealing with what they are doing, why they are doing it, and how they decided on their activity. On-demand training, real-time results, ongoing recognition, and reinforcement tied to specific actions form the basis of structured reinforcement. Success lies in determining whether a person's right-now actions are value-plus or value-minus.

In terms of team communication, sensemaking is important in establishing common ground for effective communications. The team can improve its performance and individuals can work on their personal skills using three keys. The keys to improving team communication are creating a common language that drives understanding, establishing connected communications that emphasize the how and why of interacting, and structuring reinforcement to seek out and nurture value-plus actions.

Effective team communication starts with the basics. When we decode messages in order to use a common language that drives understanding and colors the actions we engage in, we have discovered sensemaking. This social activity allows us to share ideas and influence how everyone involved makes sense of an event.

Sensemaking is important for leadership, with seven properties that provide tools to understand the communication process (Mills & Mills, 2000). Those properties are social context, personal identity, retrospect, salient clues, ongoing events, plausibility, and enactment. The theory begins with social context, allowing leaders to create meaning from relationships and conversations. Personal identity defines each person's perception of their role in the group. Retrospect is about the group interpreting what has occurred in the interaction.

Next are salient cues that allow the group to move from small bits of information to full explanations. Ongoing events speak to the reality of knowing that people act and respond based on continuing change. Plausibility is the property in which the group creates stories from salient cues and ongoing events, bringing credible sense to the interaction. Finally, enactment entails taking further steps that are informed by action and learning.

Social context is especially valuable in that it allows you to delve deeply into relationships and allows you to understand the level at which the team and its members are connected. This information can assist in creating strong ties. Weigh quality versus quantity in determining how to deal with group relationships in the time we have available each day. Using sensemaking can help by focusing networking efforts to determine whether it is best to count connections or to achieve quality connections (DiMicco & Millen, 2008).

Leaders should evaluate the group members to seek out like-mindedness to help in determining whether you are forming strong or weak ties. Strong ties promote performance based on the age of the relationship, frequency of contact, emotional attachment, reciprocity, and kinship. As any given characteristic increases, the ties get stronger.

Strong ties are those that demonstrate strong investment of time and reciprocity. Barry Wellman (1997) argued that sets of actors who maintain strong ties are more likely to trust each other in knowledge sharing, behavior modeling, and in the decision-making process (Wellman & Wortley, 1990).

Absent or infrequent contact, lack of emotional closeness, and reciprocal services lead to weak ties, which are best suited for innovation (Granovetter, 1973). Many researchers believe that organizations should create as many weak ties as possible to foster open communications and innovation.

At the end of the day, people only have time and attention to handle a few strong ties. Leaders and managers should determine which are the most important and cultivate them. The organization leadership may not be able to dictate all the ties at play. It is important to understand that you may focus on strong ties, but tens or hundreds of weak ties may be in play. Understanding the importance of ties leads us to connected communications. Also, the understanding of strong and weak ties requires that there be collaboration with leaders and their teams to establish commonality.

Connected communications are face-to-face, routine discussions with your team. These are conversations that build relationships and increase social capital. Social capital refers to a network of connections between people. This network allows shared values and behavioral norms to enable social cooperation that is mutually advantageous for all parties to the interaction. According to social capital theory, society's efficiency can be improved by facilitating coordinated action. The great thing about social capital is that it allows people to create value, achieve goals, solve problems, satisfy missions, and make significant contributions to society.

Connectedness means finding people who think and act like you. Teams seek out things that bring them together in a fundamental way without being limited by dependent or external variables. The rich conversations that result from this open, interactive team building are invaluable.

Connected communications based on social capital improve leadership and management actions as those in charge start to understand what people are doing, why they are doing it, and how they decided on their approach. The shared value that comes from open, honest communication is valuable. Three things are important. First, make sure there is a deliberate process for getting the task done. Second, establish an evaluation method and use it to improve the process if necessary. Third, work to ensure current leadership styles foster good employee communications.

Satisfaction of these management considerations empowers teams with defined roles and responsibilities. This allows the team to grow and adjust to the environment. Team members can move through the roles of leader and manager based on the task at hand. This ability to adapt to internal and external forces ensures a strong team.

Communication Accommodation Theory

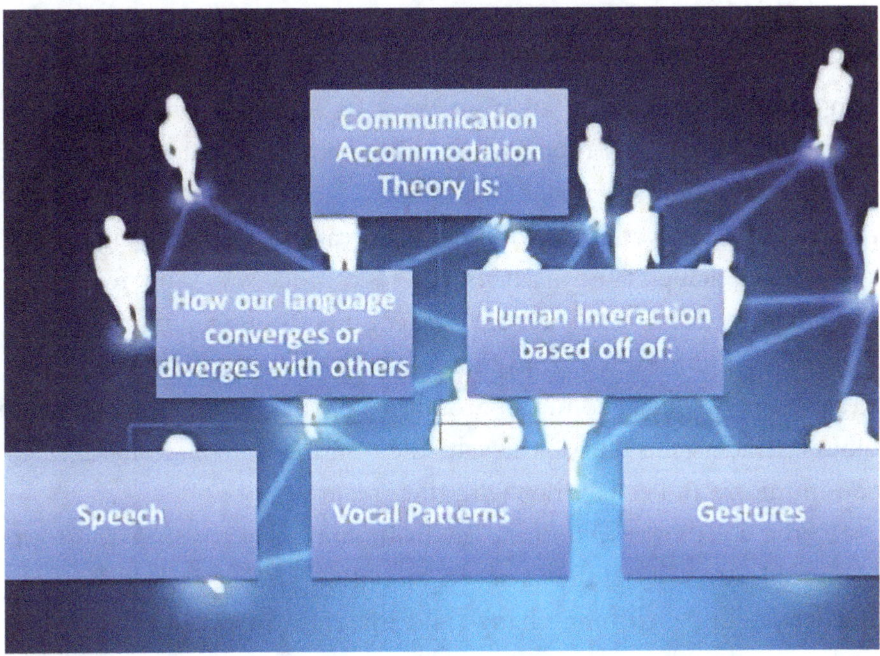

Figure 20: Communication Accommodation Theory concepts.

CAT allows us to manage our personal and social identities. According to the theory, people adjust speech, vocal patterns, and gestures to help promote mutual understanding in communication (Gallois & Giles, 2015). CAT helps us examine how to emphasize or minimize the differences between ourselves and others during verbal and non-verbal interactions. Language, context, identity, and intergroup and interpersonal factors are used in this theory to make interaction adjustments. Interpersonal control, interpretability, discourse management, and emotional expression are CAT strategies. There are also several supporting approaches that can help manage communication and adjust to receiver reaction including organizational dynamics, active listening, developing the leader within, style diversity, and ongoing self-assessment.

CAT is the way we emphasize or minimize verbal and non-verbal interaction differences as we adjust to other people. Convergence and divergence are accommodation processes used in CAT (Ayoko, Härtel, & Callan, 2002). Convergence is the way people adapt to communicative behaviors to reduce social differences. People highlight speech and non-verbal differences to arrive at ways to adjust for success. People can accommodate too much when using convergence and, when that happens, they may seem condescending.

Leaders can reverse communication breakdowns by managing discourse and achieving consensus on task processes. One researcher (Ayoko et al., 2002) studied managing conflict, finding in part that productive conflict resulted from increased use of discourse management strategies that sought common ground to repair communication roadblocks. Leaders should use the valuable resources provided in CAT to communicate and collaborate with their teams.

In the collaborative training environment, leaders adjust to group communication. This allows accommodation and flexibility that lead to effective information exchange and increased understanding. Great leaders are flexible communicators, listening and learning on the fly to adjust to each participant's emotions, risk, and feedback to get the most out of the interaction. They tailor their approach to the group atmosphere and take note of challenges based on the location or time of the interaction.

These actions must be taken with care because communication adjustments gone wrong can lead to problematic, adversarial, or dissatisfying experiences. Also, leaders who try to make the adjustments mentioned without engaging their people are almost certain to find limitations in the pursuit of success.

CAT promotes success in making these adjustments as we consider the many ways personal and social identity come into play (Giles, 2008). According to the theory, people accommodate communication partners by trying to strengthen interactions with others during various activities such as social encounters, group projects, or negotiations (Gallois & Giles, 2015). We all minimize or emphasize differences with interaction partners and CAT assists with these verbal and non-verbal challenges.

In group settings, CAT is used to ensure collective comprehension. Facilitators of group interactions should be flexible and willing to change the terms or phrases used. They may also need to change the tempo of the presentation, employ repetition to drive home a point, or change the rate of their speech.

A range of CAT strategies is available for team building from interpersonal control to interpretability to discourse management to emotional expression. For instance, one way to enhance communication abilities is through interpersonal control, which determines how much the sender controls the receiver or how one person in an interaction controls the other. Sender and receiver roles change during communication activities and interpersonal control is a way of managing or regulating another's thoughts, feelings, or actions (Stets, 1991).

The next communication enhancement is interpretability, a strategy that can be used to give the receiver additional help in understanding the message (Jones, Woodhouse, & Rowe, 2007). Communicators work with the group using visual cues, emotions, and other characteristics of the receiver to ensure that the message is delivered, and that feedback can begin.

With discourse management, we organize the information in the best way for our audience, making sure to repair any difficulties or breaks in the communication. Work to find common ground where group communication will be most effective.

Finally, emotional expression is just what it sounds like. It is how people express, regulate, experience, and influence emotions. This requires understanding and then managing our emotions and the emotions of others during a communicative interaction. Emotional expressions are observable, and they take the form of verbal and non-verbal behaviors, including audible sounds, facial movements, and obvious emotional reactions such as laughing, crying, smiling, or scowling.

The table on the next page examines CAT strategies as they relate to receiver activity levels that are relevant for group communication. The information is helpful in identifying effective and ineffective activities.

Sender-receiver Relationships – Activity Comparisons			
	Receiver Activity Level: How much does receiver engage with message and sender?		
Strategy	**High**	**Moderate**	**Low**
Interpersonal Control	• Emphasis on personal power or Position • Too formal • Lack of connection to or acceptance of the message	• Genuinely interested in the message • Participates in the feedback • Polite • Respectful • Encouraging	• In awe of the sender • Failure to share information or feedback • Surrenders too much authority to the sender
Interpretability	• Vague or ambiguous responses • Confusing or inaccurate information • No explanations	• Clear, direct, honest • Straightforward and to the point • Plenty of explanations • Verify understanding of the message	• The topic is too simple to hold your interest • Being "talked down to." • Feeling of inferiority
Discourse Management	• Dominate the conversation • Fails to listen • Does not let others speak	• Ask questions • Ask for opinions • Open to new ideas and topics • Listen first, talk second • "Chat" relationship	• Responds only when asked • Allows sender to determine what is discussed
Emotional Expression	• Hostile • Unsupportive	• Show empathy • Establish caring interaction • Give message reassurances	• Too much sympathy • Lack of real information exchange

Figure 21: Adapted from "Coding System for Communication Strategies," Effective nurse parent communication: A study of parents' perceptions in the NICU environment. (Jones et al., 2007, pp., p 209) (Brown, 2017)

CAT strategies facilitate collaboration and assist with adjusting communication based on the reaction of the receiver. There are several approaches that support CAT in sharing information with the team.

Constant efforts and adjustments to communicate with the team and to get people to collaborate create good organizational dynamics. A good start is active listening that ensures the leader is constantly tuned in to use feedback and visual and verbal cues to adjust. Energize the leader within by modeling the appropriate behavior to establish positive norms, creating freedom of expression in team members, and ensuring clear expectations throughout teams. Leaders can engage in style diversity to ensure a collaborative, open, and creative culture. They work to ensure ongoing self-assessment to examine how well the team is functioning and determine what might interfere with effectiveness.

Ensure active listening by using effective listening techniques such as questioning, paraphrasing, and summarizing to encourage conversation about ideas.

Energize the leader within by modeling behavior and establishing norms. Team members feel free to express their feelings about the tasks and to comment on the group's operation. There are few hidden agendas when people are truly energized. There is an added benefit in that this kind of empowerment allows communication to take place outside of meetings. There are clear expectations about the roles played by each team member. When action is taken, clear assignments are made, accepted, and carried out. Finally, work is fairly distributed among team members.

Engage in style diversity because the team has a broad spectrum of team-player types. This includes members who emphasize attention to task, goal setting, focus on process, and questions about how the team is functioning.

Ensure ongoing self-assessment for individuals and for the team. Periodically, the team stops to examine how well it is functioning and what may be interfering with its effectiveness.

CAT strategies can now be combined with the kind of trust that is essential in organizations.

LMX Theory addresses, in part, intentions on the part of participants in work relationships. We can learn more by studying Edwin Locke, who was an ardent critic of behaviorism. His 1964 doctoral dissertation was based on experiments testing Ryan's hypothesis regarding the effect of intentions. Latham recounts the results (1965).

The culmination of Locke's experiments led to three propositions that would subsequently lead to the development of goal setting theory in 1990: (1) Specific high goals lead to higher performance than no goals or even an abstract goal such as "do your best"; (2) given goal commitment, the higher the goal the higher the performance, and (3) variables such as monetary incentives, participation in decision making, feedback, or knowledge of results affect performance only to the extent that they lead to the setting of and commitment to specific high goals. In short, goals have the effect of directing attention and action (choice), mobilizing energy expenditure or effort, prolonging effort over time (persistence), and motivating the individual to develop relevant strategies (cognition) for goal attainment. Given goal commitment, job performance improves because the goal provides a regulatory mechanism that allows the employee to observe, monitor, subjectively evaluate, and adjust job behavior to attain the goal. Goal setting taps a fundamental attribute of human behavior, namely, goal directedness (Latham, 2012, pp. 53-54).

4

Understanding Team Dynamics

When we examine team dynamics and how relationships are created and nurtured, there are two things on which we need to focus. First, how are people treated individually and as members of the team? Second, how do people *believe* they are treated individually and as members of the team? Both are important considerations.

Understanding your team starts with helping everyone move through the five stages of conflict: forming, storming, norming, performing, and adjourning (Tuckman & Jensen, 2010). In reality, leaders come and go at different times in this process, unless they are starting up a team from scratch. The leader must have the ability to identify these stages and interact effectively regardless of where the team is in the process. Even if a leader comes in at some point in this five-stage process, storming is still a critical stage. Storming is the stage where conflict grows. Brainstorming and other deliberations increase in intensity, and teams need to manage and attempt to resolve conflict. This is not just the leader's responsibility. Traditionally, it has been left to the leader, but LMX Theory tells us that it should be a collaborative effort.

An effective collaborative effort can create great interactions that lead us to concentrate on creating interdependence and to a sense of belonging for all team members. This is done by demonstrating the value and responsibility of each member. Giving each member a sense of ownership empowers them to participate fully in team activities and/or decisions. This can in turn improve the give and take required to nurture cohesive teams.

The work involved here discusses shared understanding in a lot of ways that in turn lead us to the importance of a shared team purpose. Full participation in team goals that are well stated can improve both the deliberations on various issues and the decision-making process. Creating an understandable shared purpose is a requirement for effective group interactions.

Group interactions often reveal incompatibility between people as we discover two dimensions that characterize behavior: assertiveness and cooperativeness. Assertiveness is the level at which people work to satisfy personal concerns. Cooperativeness is the level at which people try to satisfy another person's concern. These dimensions clarify the approaches to managing conflict: accommodating, collaborating, avoiding, competing, and compromising (Dalal, 2017, pp. , p. 14).

Accommodating is a concept that is low on assertiveness and high on cooperativeness. Collaborating is the practice of being equally assertive and cooperative. Avoiding requires that one is neither assertive nor cooperative. Competing is being assertive but not cooperative, instead pursuing one's own concern at another's expense. Finally, compromising is being mildly assertive and cooperative, which makes it like collaboration on a low level. For instance, a person might not want to take any real risks of being either right or wrong.

Examining these approaches to managing conflict helps when getting to know your people and energizes the way that you can create and nurture great collaborations. You can get more details on managing conflict by referring to "An Exploratory Study on Conflict Management with the Perspective of Education as a Variable" (Dalal, 2017).

Understanding how to manage conflict is valuable because teams often feature diverse, complicated relationships. These relationships should strive for strong communication, a common language, and consensus about the direction of the the effort involved. All lines of communication should always be open, and organizations and their leaders must give and receive feedback. They must analyze the feedback from all sources and take the necessary actions with respect to what they learn. Good organizations and leaders ensure that every member of the team is aware of the continuing commitment to engage in conversations about the issues of the day, whether they are about tasking, performing, or maintaining a work life balance.

What Comes Next?

This chapter examines team dynamics and the vital need to create and nurture relationships. We just covered managing conflicts, ensuring collaboration, achieving shared understanding, navigating group inter-actions effectively, and ensuring continuing commitment from every-one. What comes next?

Focusing on the relationships is something that all teams – top to bottom – need to do to enhance information sharing and creativity to create a sense of belonging across the organization.

Leadership and its role in building teams is a great responsibility. In team situations, leaders are charged with finding success with a mix of points of view: the willing, the undecided, the unwilling, and the combative.

- The willing member is almost sure to do whatever the team needs whenever it is needed.
- The undecided member tends to be interested but is not sure at what level they want to participate or buy into the goal.

- The unwilling member may not be interested in success and will not exert any effort to advance the goal.
- The combative member may exhibit any of the traits of the other three, but this person is guided by their own needs, regardless of what the team needs.

So, the leader's job is to make it work. Leaders must use their skill and connection with their team to find ways to bring everyone along on the journey to success. They must find a way to show each member that there is a benefit to their participation and buy-in, no matter how easy or hard the journey might be. As we continue to discuss this kind of team building, leaders must remember that *The RFL Process* is about *collaborating*. The leader is not expected to go it alone. In fact, the process shows how invaluable collaboration can be.

One way to bring people together is to understand the science of leading. Of course, we could use Maslow's Hierarchy of Needs (Maslow 1970) or McGregor's Theory X and Theory Y (McGregor). However, the work of Maslow and McGregor came under scrutiny due to a perceived lack of available data. The criticisms of Maslow's and McGregor's theories were that there was no supporting data available.

Lyman Porter supported their work with theory-driven empirical research analyzing industry competition to develop business strategies using five forces (Porter and Donthu 2008, Porter 2008). Three of the five forces (the nature of rivalry, new entrants, and substitutes) involve competitors and the other two forces are customers and suppliers. Porter conducted five studies, largely using Maslow's theory as a framework. Porter was explaining organizational dynamics as forces that can significantly impact a company's performance in an industry. Maslow's work allowed Porter to view these forces from a humanistic point of view.

The competing theories and research here suggest a focus on the work of Gary P. Latham. Latham used Porter's work to develop an assessment of motivation, using a proficiency scale to allow people to rate the importance of characteristics present in their job as well as how much of each characteristic they would prefer to have in the job. His work was published in Work Motivation: History, Theory, Research, and Practice (Latham 2007). In 1961 Porter conducted a study of foremen and mid-level managers of three different companies, finding that the highest order need, self-actualization, is the most critical of those studied, in terms of both perceived deficiency in fulfillment and perceived importance to the individual (Mowday, Steers et al. 1979, Latham 2007).

Latham gives us a useful examination of the history and development of motivation in the workplace. His pillars define workplace motivation by addressing the characteristics involved in people's choice, effort, and persistence. In Latham's view, motivation is a crucial requirement for training and is a core competency of leadership. He argues that the importance of galvanizing and inspiring people to exert effort is vital to training. Further, training is vital to effective leadership in terms of motivating people to commit to and persist in the pursuit of an organization's values or goals.

Latham's "Choice" means the leader is either getting people to decide on actions on their own or the leader is making a case for why people should take a recommended course of action. "Effort" relates to the amount of energy a person gives to an initiative. We know that a motivational leader can inspire the kind of adrenaline in a person that allows them to move past their hesitations, find energy where there is none, and believe even if they don't know why they believe. "Persistence" is about helping people keep trying when they don't believe their effort and energy will be enough to take a particular course of action.

By setting high goals that lead to change or progress that is important, attainable, and sustainable, leaders and their teams can achieve the shared understanding that builds relationships. The leader must recognize their own emotions to be effective at interacting with their team. This is consistent with good principles of emotional intelligence. These actions provide opportunities to deliver value to each party involved in the process and to achieve buy-in through collaboration. True engagement comes when collaboration creates effective interaction that promotes team building and objective satisfaction.

Reputation Management

This kind of engagement has the potential to improve organizational culture. In turn, we know that organizational culture affects the workforce as well as the bottom line. Now, we are focusing on reputation management to connect with people and perform well.

Good reputation management starts with crafting and distributing key messages to your people, the most important audience, as the foundation of successful internal and corporate communications. Company values and a solid brand voice are crucial to shaping and maintaining core values and behaviors that support a thriving culture. Good reputation management requires that the culture and the brand are clear in all communications and activities.

Below are some "outside of the box" ideas to help leadership with crafting the corporate reputation and connecting with the workforce:

- Clearly describe the benefits your organization stands to gain from actively addressing culture change (or adjustment).

- Tie new/adjusted core values directly to the annual climate survey.
- Conduct All hands meetings without slides.
- Fill common areas with large displays of information, preferably that highlight your people doing their jobs (infographics) .
- Conduct company recreation or holiday events with activities and teams named after values.
- Survey employees about behaviors that are conducive to company values.
- Act on feedback from employees about how to show adherence to values; define behaviors.
- Use core values in hiring and performance appraisals.
- Determine and publish keys to success for the team.
- Engage leadership at all levels.
- Set realistic time horizons for change.
- Take an innovative approach to create programs for your people to achieve work-life balance (you may have to do it with no budget).

These efforts work best when leaders and their teams practice good EI. This means the leader must teach, or verify, that the EI principles are clear to everyone. Then leaders can focus on the strengths and weaknesses that are created by their emotions and make sure they are doing the same for those they lead. People often make decisions based on their emotions, so understanding and controlling emotions is vital.

This is a way to conduct quality interactions with others. Identify the value available to each party and then use two-way communication to achieve shared understanding and achieve buy-in. EI allows leaders to conduct effective communication with the team as it promotes getting to know themselves and their team members. This improves the ability to be impartial and to listen for ideas, not just words.

Understanding the team, conducting good group interactions, improving your culture, and using EI to the best advantage are all good for leading. However, do you remember how this chapter started? The company and its leaders cannot stop here. They must address the second issue raised in this chapter: how do people *believe* they are treated individually and as members of the team?

This is an issue where engagement with the workforce is important. For example, a 2012 study (Stillman) found a large degree of disagreement between leaders and members in the way each group views engagement. Leaders thought the message was getting through and people were being taken care of. Middle management and human resources disagreed that the communication and service was strong in both directions. And employees said they wanted feedback that they were not getting. The survey reflects disconnects in communication, understanding, perspective, and feedback that can weaken an organization. So, the required task is to find out how to measure and then take action to get everyone on the same page.

The study results demonstrate that leaders need to engage with team members to make sure there is a common perspective about work tasks, recognition, and other issues. Effective engagement requires not being too busy or distracted to be in touch with the ongoing experiences of their team members. Lack of engagement robs leaders of the chance to get a real view of daily operations, thoughts, and stressors. Leaders must move through the organization frequently and take the time to ask people what they are doing and why. Make time for one-on-one engagements to allow for the best two-way communication in real time.

In today's world, we sometimes see organizations that have a crisis and they react with a safety or security "stand down" to address the issues. For instance, when the military identified a perceived problem with support for white supremacy in its ranks as the nation was coming out of COVID, they ordered a stand down. The secretary of Defense provided a video denouncing any improper treatment of people and reinforcing the oath of office for military and civil servants. The video was played at all locations followed by focus groups. There should have been two-way communication in these focus groups, but did all organizations really achieve that? Did the stand down achieve EI success? We may never know.

So let's talk about trust. Trust is created and nurtured by sharing conversations and emotions in the team. Stephen Covey, American educator, author, and keynote speaker, said, "Trust is the highest form of human motivation. It brings out the very best in people (Frank Messina, 2011, p. 219)." Trust can eliminate or minimize uncertainty for communicating parties because it allows each party to believe that the other will behave in a way that is beneficial. When the result of the communication is shared value and common understanding, a bond is created.

Why discuss trust within a reputation management section? Organizations that have the trust of their members are blessed with the best spokespersons available. People who trust in their organization and a feel a real sense of belonging will sing your praises without being asked. That is valuable.

When we think about team dynamics, it is often about how people are treated AND how they think they are treated. C.A. O'Reilly (1991) found that the majority of organizational behavior studies focus on the dominant theories of goal setting and equity. Latham advances the notion that organizational justice principles are as much about leadership as they are about employee motivation. There are two considerations: (1) Distributive justice focuses on what was distributed, who it was distributed to, and who received what distribution; and (2) Procedural justice is concerned with whether there are procedures, processes, or systems in place for determining what was distributed to whom.

5

Developing Motivationally Intelligent Teams

Building Motivationally Intelligent Teams is about combining coaching and mentoring techniques for the best results. These teams feature partnerships that pursue team and individual goals with equal importance.

Figure 22: Building Motivationally Intelligent Teams.

I value creative thinking and interactive communication with people that features feedback. I strive for flexibility in my approach to allow me to tailor my efforts to students, employees, and or athletes of various backgrounds. When teaching, I will use grading rubrics to ensure commonality in language, approach, and objectives at all part of the education process.

But let's focus on the teaching aspect. I am currently a public administration adjunct with Florida Tech, a research university, primarily teaching courses online. I previously taught at Florida International University, Old Dominion University, at the University of Maryland University College (now University of Maryland Global Campus), and at Southern Illinois University at Carbondale (student teaching).

- Creative thinking is important so I can allow students to think outside the box.
    - This is a way to increase innovation and find novel ways that students can demonstrate their grasp of the educational objectives.
    - It allows them to grow.
- Interactive communication sparks robust relationships with my students.
    - The goal is to make sure the students can apply what they learn in my class across educational pursuits and in life.
    - I want to break down barriers to learning and enhance transference of knowledge in students.

- I practice teaching flexibility to allow for social and emotional development of all students.
    - It ensures that I am aware of effective school environments and that students can be themselves and feel comfortable sharing their feelings and experiences.
- The grading rubrics help students keep track of objectives, manage expectations, and see the big picture.
    - These are invaluable when students are checking their papers for accuracy.
    - They also prove helpful when a student, or an administrator, has a conflict about a grade.
    - They protect and help everyone.

Define Your Team

I identify team roles as leader, manager, and team member. This is important because any member might fill any role at any time. Role changes can happen because of a promotion for demotion, assignment on a special project, or in response to a crisis. The leader is the person at the head of the organization or section who has the final vote, say, or decision. The manager is the liaison between the leader and the team.

The team members are the people who perform the lion's share of the actual work, implementing plans and affecting change based on the stated course of action. In a lot of ways, the team members have the most power by virtue of their direct ability to influence the work in one way or another. I recommend that leaders keep in mind that these roles are always at play and try to identify when role definition or revision is required. Consistent with the collaborative approach, this analysis should be done by the team, or by some part of it.

Leaders must develop effective traits that will create positive partnerships and work ethic in business environments, highlighting pertinent topics such as Engaged Interaction, team communication, and work motivation. Everyone involved in leader and team development should understand and apply active listening techniques such as questioning, paraphrasing, and summarizing to exchange ideas.

Participants should also engage in style diversity to ensure an open and creative culture that is collaborative. Ongoing self-assessment ensures that participants examine how well the team is functioning and determine what might interfere with effectiveness.

Task Analyzability

Perrow defines task analyzability as the way that individuals are able to respond to problems encountered in the process of task completion (1967). This analyzability is helpful due to the predetermined responses to potential problems or to the use of well-known procedures. This certainty moves the group to outcomes that can be easily understood. There are four areas in which task analyzability can provide information (Withey, Daft, & Cooper, 1983):

- Clear definitions for accomplishing the major types of work.
- Clearly defined and available body of knowledge.
- Clear sequence of steps for tasks.
- Reliance on policy and procedures.

Task analyzability is about making a critical analysis of activities to determine the benefits they may deliver. There are additional task analyzability questions that can deliver helpful information:

- Is there a clear way to do the major types of work (conduct activities)?
- Is there a clearly defined body of knowledge matter available?
- Is there an understandable sequence of steps to follow?
- Is there actual reliance on established procedures and practices?

The way organizations address projects and associated tasks should be routine so that everyone has a common understanding (Welker, 2004). This relates to task analyzability and task variety (Daft & Macintosh, 1981). Task analyzability, as mentioned earlier, reduces the task to standard steps. Task variety is about how often new or unexpected events become part of the process. High task analyzability creates a need to use standardized procedures or technical knowledge.

When the task cannot be fully analyzed, the team must resort to judgment, intuition, and experience of its members. Experts say that routine tasks are low in variety and high in analyzability and that non-routine tasks are high in variety and low in analyzability. There is little complexity in routine tasks, and it is easy to plan these in advance. There is high analyzability that allows the team to rely on detailed rules and procedures. There is, of course, greater uncertainty with non-routine tasks that does not allow preplanning (Tushman & Nadler, 1978).

Working to add variety and analyzability to tasks involves bringing clarity to the effort. Start with what you know and then list what you need to complete the project. Pay careful attention to the problems or delays that the team might face. Once you have paid attention to all of that, assign tasks to your team members.

Once tasks are assigned, make sure that you take care of accountability. Each person is accountable to the team for their assignment. Create an environment where each person understands that asking for help is a positive trait, not a negative one. If they find the task is too much for them to handle, they should feel free to make it known and they should do so before the task is due for completion.

An open and honest dialogue allows people to seek help and work together in a collaborative environment where successes and failures contribute to shared ideas, improved skills, and project completion. This is done by effectively defining goals up front, identifying the related tasks, creating a timeline for completion, identifying required resources, enlisting help when necessary, and welcoming feedback throughout the life of the project or event. A good project review after you're done can help benchmark what works and what doesn't. This is crucial for team success in the next endeavor.

Asking Tough Questions

Now it's time to ask the tough individual and team questions that will reveal characteristics – good and bad – of your team and its members. Individuals will want to examine how they see themselves personally and professionally. Two questions are initially important. How much control do they think they have over organizational actions and personal actions? Do they know what to do next?

From a team standpoint, the questioning phase attempts to determine whether the organization has a clear purpose, clear roles, and reasonable work assignments. Does the team provide room for its members to grow? Does the team have a consistency of effort and strong internal communications?

Let's identify the needs of teams and individuals based on the questions for individuals and teams in the table below.

Tough Questions	
Individual	**Team**
Who am I and what do I want personally and professionally?	Do we have a clear purpose?
What actions do I control?	Do we have clear roles and reasonable work assignments?
What should I be doing now?	Do we provide room for our team members to grow?
	Do we have a consistency of effort and strong internal communications?

Figure 23: Asking tough questions for individuals and teams.

The answers to these questions are crucial to building a successful plan. The roles have already been defined, so you may have to make some minor adjustments to get everything to fit together for your team. Then you can take all the information you've gathered and craft a plan for success that will serve your team well today, tomorrow, and in the future.

These are very tough questions. Leaders need to ask them and create an environment where anyone on the team can ask these questions at any point in the process. You need people who are free to play "devil's advocate."

The devil's advocate is going to disagree with everything you want to do. In extreme cases the devil's advocate will give you an example of a negative outcome or tell you how the success you find in the short term will turn out to be failure in the long term. This can be unnerving and annoying, but it is human nature. It is also good practice for making sure you consider the "cons" of each course of action before making a final decision.

The devil's advocate forces the team to listen to alternate points of view. This information can uncover new and different insights than were considered earlier in the deliberations. As you and the group get exposed to these alternate ideas and viewpoints, everyone is forced to explain their position, defend the decision, or rethink the path the group is on. Of course, you've considered alternate solutions and outcomes, but the devil's advocate tends to suggest the darkest days and the worst outcomes for your consideration.

The person who fills the devil's advocate role may do it for a variety of reasons. They may just want to challenge the course that the group is on. They may truly have reservations about the deliberations and the impending decision. They may want to offer an alternative viewpoint to assess everyone's conviction in terms of the proposed course of action. They may, in fact, be a bad person who thinks the worst and wants the worst.

Whatever the case, this is a necessary part of group dynamics. This causes a pro versus con discussion that can be rich and rewarding, though it might be annoying at the same time.

The key to a group's ability to handle this discourse well in groups is that when the rationale for the decision has been made sufficiently to satisfy the group or the decision maker, it is necessary to concede the argument or discussion and move on to actions. A stalemate does no one any good, especially if injured feelings remain.

Three quotes are presented here to drive home the benefit of the devil's advocate:

- *Honest disagreement is often a good sign of progress.*
  - Mahatma Ghandi, Indian political and spiritual leader (1869 – 1948).
- *If everyone is thinking alike, then someone isn't thinking.*
  - George S. Patton, American hero and Army general officer (1885 – 1945).
- *A genuine leader is not a searcher for consensus but a molder of consensus.*
  - Dr. Martin Luther King Jr., American Baptist minister and activist and Civil Rights Movement leader (1929 – 1968).

Armed with numerous ways to refine your team, you can determine how to serve both the individual and the group effectively. Design a plan that will guide the journey to success and consistent improvement.

Ready to Lead

Now you are equipped with great tools to apply *The RFL Process* to collaborative leadership training. The Motivationally Intelligent Leader minimizes bias, works to avoid fatigue, and is optimistic about acting.

Analyze Without Bias: Analyze the situation and the way ahead and think about the desired end state. The relationship between these items is important in helping to determine what is necessary to proceed. Keep an open mind and be prepared in case the outcome is not what you expected. Listening to different viewpoints is very important in mitigating bias.

Momentum without Fatigue: Decide and move out, attacking the solution with conviction and creating momentum that will take the team to a successful conclusion. The relationship you build before trouble is the relationship you will nurture in good times. Show that you trust the team and stay connected until everyone is on the same page: achieving.

Action without Discouragement: Always take action to implement the decisions that have been made. Make the necessary course corrections along the way. Overall, stay the course to show confidence in the process that allowed you to find the way ahead.

The leader's actions, decisions, and relationships should be such that they think about others first, the goal or mission second, and themselves third. Commit to leadership and be constant in that commitment.

Now, we see that Motivationally Intelligent Teams are equipped to master these characteristics (traits): emotional stability, interaction flexibility, and situational command. Each has a focus area and establishes the way the leader applies actions or resources based on analysis, momentum, and action. Finally, here is a suggestion of the kind of qualities that are important to achieving success or to recruiting people to your team. Please feel free to add to, change, or delete these qualities so that they are best suited for your team and your challenge.

Motivational Intelligent Leadership Characteristics			
Trait	**Focus Area**	**Leadership Application for Engaging Your Team**	**Best Quality for Success or Recruitment**
Emotional Stability	Leader-Focused	**Analysis Without Bias:** Assess leader skills *without judging*. **Momentum Without Fatigue:** *Stay engaged* as long needed to complete the mission. **Action Without Discouragement:** *Think positively* even when facing disappointments or setbacks.	• Confidence • Empathy • Self-Control • Trust
Interaction Flexibility	Member-Focused	**Analysis Without Bias:** Assess member skills *without judging*. **Momentum Without Fatigue:** *Focus participation* on moving the goal. **Action Without Discouragement:** *Think positively* even when facing disappointments or setbacks.	• Commitment • Collaboration • Cooperation • Information Sharing • Innovation • Networking
Situational Command	Group-Focused	**Analysis Without Bias:** Assess collective group skills *without judging*. **Momentum Without Fatigue:** *Keep the group on the same page* toward mission completion. **Action Without Discouragement:** *Use team building activities* to foster collaboration and overcome disappointments or setbacks.	• Discipline • Empowerment • Role Definition • Innovation • Networking • Trust

Figure 24: Characteristics of Motivationally Intelligent Leadership (revised April 23, 2023). (Brown SR, 2017, P.113)

Of course, there is more to leadership than this chart, but you inspire people by being calm in chaos, deliberate when there is doubt, and caring when there is trouble. Let's take a closer look at how this chart can lead to effectiveness. Many case studies about leadership point to failing grades in taking care of people, symbolized by the emphasis on "F" in the chart below. A partial list of the reasons is provided below.

- **<u>Emotional Stability</u>**
  - *F*ighting change.
  - *F*ocusing solely on the big picture.
- **<u>Interaction Flexibility</u>**
  - *F*ailing to find dedicated time for the team to communicate.
  - *F*rustration caused by the existence of a "do as I say, not as I do" environment.
- **<u>Situational Command</u>**
  - *F*luctuating or nonexistent team goals, roles, and responsibilities.
  - *F*orgetting the importance of feedback and delegation.

A Motivationally Intelligent Team can address the principles of emotional stability, interaction flexibility, and situational command that are in the previous table. This is a formula for success.

Emotional stability is focused on the leader. Team members may resist a necessary change, so the leader must be firm and fair in getting people to adjust and agree. Leaders must see the big picture, explain it to the team, and seek buy in. It is even more important that leaders find ways to break the whole into manageable parts. This allows the team to work on the task in reasonable segments for maximum efficiency.

While the team adjusts to change and to working within the big picture, the leader should be evaluating their own skills and emotional make up as they relate to the emotions of others. Leaders must stay engaged with the interaction or other activity and be committed as long as is necessary to achieve mission success. Leaders should always strive to think positively when facing disappointments or setbacks.

Team members should practice interaction flexibility as the leader works to create and nurture great relationships with the whole team. More than just talking with team members, leaders must find dedicated time to communicate one-on-one whenever possible. Leaders should know that many team members want more than superficial conversations. Getting to know each other builds trust and confidence within the team. In addition to communicating well, team members want leaders who are part of the team; not above it. People quickly become frustrated with leaders who maintain a "do as I say, not as I do" environment.

Norms and values must apply to every member of the team. Communication and fair inclusion in the way the organization is managed will help people adjust to the leader as they evaluate their own skills. As this team building happens, organizations must ensure that training or professional development is readily available. Schedule and conduct meaningful activities that grow your people and create momentum that ensures consistent pursuit of the organization's goal. When there are disappointments or setbacks, team members should try to work with the leader to think positively about the possibility that there are better days ahead.

Situational command is group-focused and involves the team's ability to control the situation at hand, or to at least be composed enough to think clearly about how to address the next steps. Controlling the situation and taking on challenges requires solid team goals, roles, and responsibilities. Everyone must know what to do and who is accountable for each task, and feedback and delegation are additional keys to situational command. Feedback communicates the plusses and minuses of goal achievement and thus allows the necessary changes or course corrections to stay on target for mission success. Delegation allows team members to take control of new and challenging tasks and to stretch their capabilities. The leader benefits from allowing people to have greater responsibility and, possibly, to train their future replacement.

A constant evaluation of individual and group skills creates working relationships where people can achieve based on their strengths and develop by improving their weaknesses. Situational command allows leaders and managers to employ the buddy system for maximum efficiency. A person who is not the greatest writer can be paired with someone who needs better time management. Now they can balance each person's strengths and weaknesses in an effort to find success. Partnering often helps when there are difficulties at work, because people are already paired up and they may be able to help each other.

As teams work through stability, flexibility, and command issues, they should take three more steps that will aid success. First, applaud small wins to keep individuals and the group excited about their task. Second, encourage innovation even if it throws the organization off course a bit. Sometimes it is important to take a chance on something new because failures might happen even if you do not risk a new approach. Third, set and celebrate milestones. Don't just set one target for the end of the journey, establish points of success where the team can clearly see that they are progressing toward the goal. This keeps people motivated.

Don't Forget Digital Capabilities

As you work with your team, take advantage of digital applications whenever you can. COVID-19, and the world's recovery from it, has driven the debate about where people work. There are many conversations and/or disagreements about on-site versus remote versus hybrid work. Digital applications can reduce the emphasis on where people work. For instance, coworking and desk sharing have been increasing in popularity for several years. At the height of COVID-19, digital methods allowed dispersed operations where people can create, innovate, network, and even freelance.

Today's organizations should consider the possibilities that exist in technology that remove the limits of where, when, and how work can be done (Leclercq-Vandelannoitte & Isaac, 2016). Leaders and managers should be focused on ways to assess how to take advantage of digital offices and processes. Digitally savvy companies may in fact have the upper hand in hiring the best and brightest. This is a growing, exciting area of discovery for companies that want to move into the future.

Using digital resources is enhanced when there is trust. When organizations and leaders examine today's operations that have been drastically altered since COVID-19, they are confronted with many challenges of adapting employees, business operations, productivity levels, technology, and more to meet this increased demand in work life balance and work location. Through these challenges, companies and employees engaged in new or changed understanding and desires in their work-life relationship.

Trust is often a major issue at stake in these deliberations, however, employers and those they lead do not always recognize that the discussion is not totally about location. These interactions have changed because the world is changing and because more workers are seeking win-win situations instead of the traditional "organization first and only" approach. There are numerous conversations and social media posts about the ways in which trust is very often the driver in these situations.

Open and honest communications in these areas that focus on achieving trustworthiness and improving performance must focus equally on benefits gained and risks involved. Focus on factors that are key to ensuring good decision-making: productivity, employee risk, achievement, and accountability. Success relies on achieving the best possible outcome with a minimum of input. Keep in mind that performance is based on output only, so organizations and leaders might do well to focus more on productivity. Productivity is activity designed to understand the value of inputs, outputs, and return on investments (Brown Sr., 2021).

The bottom line is to find ways to assess factors that are important to team members, such as flexibility, enhanced work-life balance, and worker independence. These factors can help people deal with family health and safety and other considerations. Team members can be more productive when these stressors are mitigated or reduced.

So, whether your organization is traditional or digitally focused or some combination, there are constants for you to consider. Also, these considerations should be covered in the collaborative training we are addressing in this work. All of the knowledge in this chapter, and in this book, relies on a collaborative, open communication that is woven into the organization's culture.

You can't change yesterday, so you should focus on making tomorrow better. Today is an opportunity and tomorrow is a challenge, so enjoy the journey to achieving *Motivationally Intelligent Teams* through **The RFL Process**.

Motivationally intelligent leaders should always be interested in what motivates their team. Robert and Joyce Hogan developed Socioanalytic Theory (2001). The theory asserts that people are constantly in need of either getting along or getting ahead. They are pursuing getting along when they pursue acceptance, approval, and popularity. Getting ahead involves the need for power, control, and status. Interpersonal relationships are inherently problematic because of the dichotomy of actions. One can solve the problem of getting along by simply acting in a way that would avoid disapproval. However, to get ahead one may need to adopt more active and manipulative forms of self-presentation.

6 |

A Primer in Leadership Styles

This chapter will give you good information for training great teams. We will continue examining the importance of trust. The chapter also provides tools that can be used to create and nurture trust.

Before continuing the exploration of trust, we must understand that leader and team training in a collaborative environment rely on situational leadership.

Situational leadership

When using situational leadership theory, the leader uses cues in the situation and adapts the style for the best result. The cues are typically the type of task, the kind of group, the timeline, and other factors that would indicate how to best get the job done. Management experts Paul Hersey and Ken Blanchard developed this theory in 1969 (Bates, 2016, p. 44), stating that the best leaders employ a range of different styles depending on the environment. In other words, the leader adjusts the level of being direct or supportive based on the situation of subordinates and their level of commitment or motivation (Deshwal & Ali, 2020, p. 40).

Situational leadership is also a way to take advantage of the benefits of collaborative training. For instance, a 2015 study in Norway analyzed the importance of basing situational leadership predictions on a combination of a leader rating of follower competence and commitment and a follower self-rating. The study argued that this combination produced an effective way to measure follower competence and commitment. "[Situational leadership theory] predictions are more likely to hold when leader rating and follower self-rating are congruent, rather than leader rating alone,… (Thompson & Glasø, 2015)."

This is another resource for organizations addressing the on-site versus remote versus hybrid work location issue mentioned in the last chapter. Leaders may be affected by negative perceptions of individual performance because it can be difficult or impossible to observe or monitor members working when you cannot see them, or when they do not share your work location. Leaders traditionally want to observe their workers in person, manipulating co-worker interactions and relationships. Leaders may also have a pessimistic view of how available and attentive workers are throughout the course of the day. There may also be a history of workers not responding when there is an urgent or short notice task that must be done. When this is the case, there should be standard organizational practices that are helpful to both sides.

For organizations focused on on-site work, it is important to be clear about the reasons for the decision. Following the COVID crisis, many organizations have successfully returned to on-site work , stating either "that's what we prefer" or "that's the way it used to be" as their reasoning. It is important that the organization leadership is honest with themselves about why this is the best solution. My belief is that it is very often just about the level of trust that exists between the organization, the leaders, and the members. If that is the case, this should be addressed openly.

I can say from experience that some requirements for "return to the office" are just preference or desire to return to the past and are lacking an understanding of the importance of engaging with your team before making a final decision. One concern I have experienced is that "we cannot be sure they are working if we do not see them." I will tell you that they can fool you about whether they are working, even if you are standing right in front of them. This has happened to me. Also, if you trust a person and they show accountability to you, there can be options for their work location.

Two other concerns I have heard are that "teams are more effective when they are face-to-face," and "I can call an impromptu meeting to fix an issue if everyone is in the office." I have personally been in organizations where these kinds of meetings do not exist. Yes, there is a regular staff meeting, but the organization is not always engaging face-to-face. There is often a mix of in person and virtual attendees. Finally, that impromptu meeting may not happen, but not because of remote work. It could be hindered by morning traffic in some localities, or by the lunch hour, or by the crisis happening after most people have departed for the day. Or people may not be feeling well and, after COVID, the consensus is to leave the office or avoid going to the office in those situations.

In the case of remote or hybrid work, best practices that are reciprocal are outlined in a study of outcomes and facilitators for employers where the organization has a proven, formal process for selecting and preparing employees for telework and where the organization effectively manages flexible work practices (Beauregard, Basile, & Canonico, 2019, p. 1). This type of remedy relies on a culture of trustworthiness and openness that has adequate communications, IT equipment, and support. There is also benefit in having "an adapted physical workplace to allow teleworkers to work and interact with their colleagues when they come to the office (Beauregard et al., 2019, p. 42)."

The discussion here is not intended to convince anyone to choose between on-site, remote, or hybrid. I just suggest that organizations should be flexible in helping people have a balance of focus between their work life and their personal life, and that they have some choice in where and when they work. The importance of this was demonstrated in a survey that reported that 37% of employees would leave their current job in favor of one that allowed them to choose their work location at least part of the time (Gallup, 2017).

It might help organizations to think of remote and hybrid work as an investment in people to give them flexibility in the interest of improving work-life balance. Allowing either of these approaches and ensuring two-way communication with feedback helps to create and nurture trust. Culture and operations that support any of these approaches to work location can create a win-win situation for everyone involved.

Trust is a Gift

Leadership development for teams must start with an understanding of trust. Trust is a gift that someone gives you. Trust is built through effective relationships that are characterized by role definition, shared understanding, emotional intelligence, sensemaking, accommodation, empowerment, and refinement.

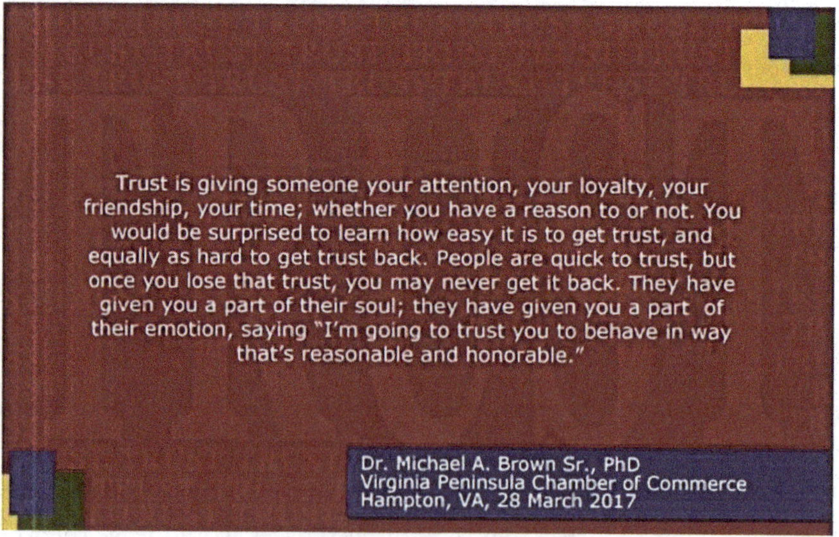

Figure 25: Trust is a gift.

Role definition: Once team roles and responsibility are defined, ensure that you train people for various roles based on current and future needs and plans. Leaders are charged to train and prepare their team for the changing nature of the world of work. Leaders should ensure that they conduct collaborative operations and training that are based on the major skills mentioned in the graphic below.

Figure 26: Leadership skill development factors.

Shared understanding: Teams can reap the benefits of setting high goals to motivate high-level achievements. A focus on need satisfaction and on creating positive energy is good for personal and team motivation. When we take care of people and there is shared understanding, we should get other benefits from the team dynamic, like exhibiting ethical and moral behavior and connecting with people in meaningful relationships. A collaborative environment with open lines of communication and plenty of feedback builds the trust that makes a team more effective. The team may be more productive based on shared understanding.

Emotional or motivational intelligence: The discussion of intelligence, emotional and/or motivational, is about each person working to understand their own emotions, the emotions of others, and about trying to adjust based on the interplay of each. In this way, we can identify and employ the value that is available to all parties to an interaction and come out of it with total buy-in. Engaged Interaction reminds us to listen, hear, and understand in full-range communications based on a mutual agreement to continue communicating until you get it right. Now the team can grow with fair-minded, dedicated participants who listen for ideas, not just words.

Sensemaking: This means decoding messages and using a common language to engage people. Team members share ideas and communicate with those around them to make sense of their social context. This facilitates trusting relationships. The collaborative communications and training between leaders and their teams ensure value-plus actions based on open and honest discussions and clear roles and responsibilities.

Accommodation: CAT teaches us to manage personal and social identity. People adjust speech, vocal patterns, and gestures to achieve mutual understanding. Then, interaction adjustments are made based on language, context, identity, and intergroup and interpersonal factors. Team efficiency comes from managing messages and the resulting reactions through organizational dynamics, active listening, developing the leader within, style diversity, and ongoing self-assessment. These things can lead to individual growth and team trust.

Empowerment: Empower your team through vision, analysis, training, motivation, and stress reduction. Teams can achieve an agreed upon end state using these tools. Together, the team dissects the whole process, develops skills, guides, and cheers people on to success. All of these approaches can make the work environment relaxing and inviting.

Refinement: Effective administration and attention to detail can accentuate the strengths, and mitigate the weaknesses, of the team and its members. The leader must understand how people form and nurture connections. This information is used to build lasting relationships within the team and to ask clarifying questions when needed. These clarifying questions, even if they must be negative in tone, will help the team to create and continue open and honest dialogue that leads to effective plans.

What we are discussing here is the formula to create Motivationally Intelligent Teams. Successful teams will be characterized by flexibility, adaptability, and relevance in pursuing organizational success. These teams tend to create effective plans that are valuable, specific, measurable, and that allow everyone to partner to reach organizational objectives. This process is about setting objectives and the general methods that can be used to achieve these objectives.

There are a variety of taxonomies for categorizing plans – by breadth, time frame, specificity, and management level. A particularly helpful way to consider different approaches is to separate them into strategic plans and tactical plans (Rawlins & Wilson, 1996, pp. , p. 63). Strategic planning is broad in scope and focused on the future. Strategic planning considers the basic nature (mission) and direction (strategy) of an organization.

Tactical planning focuses on elements of the strategic plan. It is concerned with short-term results and is much more detailed than is strategic planning. Tactical planning is the process of determining the specific operations that will achieve the broad objectives of the strategic plan.

Each organization must decide which type of plan works best. When I worked in Air Force Public Affairs, a new strategic planning approach began in the mid-1990s. Those plans established the priorities that would guide public affairs professionals as they delivered the service's messages. The strategic plan represented a roadmap that set the organization's purpose, vision, and mission to show the Public Affairs career field the big picture approach.

Next, tactical plans at headquarters down to lower levels defined the "local" approach that would keep all efforts focused. Each organization worked on their own issues, while the plans kept all actions clearly aligned with the Air Force's long-term goals and objectives. The Air Force workforce improved as day-to-day performance worked together with long-term improvements.

Each organization should attempt to build this consistency of action at all levels of their planning efforts. Just as important, it must be an integral part of any training initiative. A complete planning effort that features this approach provides a good possibility that the team will reap the benefits of personal and professional development and improvement of its players.

Knowing the members of your team and what motivates them is always important. Abraham Maslow argued that as one need is fulfilled, its strength is diminished and the strength of the next need in the hierarchy is increased. Maslow's theory had a tremendous influence on Douglas McGregor's Theory X and Theory Y (1960). McGregor viewed himself as a behavioral scientist and advanced the notion in 1957 that it was time to apply social sciences to make human organizations truly effective. McGregor based his argument on assumptions about motivation. There were criticisms that McGregor did not have enough data, but he still made assumptions about human motivation that leads to two
approaches.

Theory X: People inherently dislike work, they must be coerced or controlled to do work to achieve objectives, and they prefer to be directed.

Theory Y: People will exercise self-direction and self-control towards achieving objectives they are committed to, and people will learn to accept and seek responsibility.

How Do We Teach It?

Teaching plans set the stage for learning opportunities. ***The RFL Process*** addresses a full range of leader and member development needs. It starts with training in the overall process, demonstrating how to develop teams from the CEO to the manager to the employee. In defining the process, the plan covers EI and empathy and relates them to effective leadership behaviors.

Those who use this plan can evaluate different approaches to leadership, develop their personal style through self-assessment, and apply accountability and responsiveness to their environment. The EI teaching plan focuses on the ways people manage, or do not manage, their own emotions and the emotions of others. Empathy, leadership behavior, and LMX Theory are key parts of this teaching approach.

Leadership styles and team building are used to develop skills that are important to creating win-win situations in an organizational setting. The training also demonstrates how to create shared understanding among all participants.

Leader and team development training should address key issues and answers for collaborating. These include trustworthiness, performance, productivity, employee risk, achievement, accountability, EI, and radical change. One definition of radical change is that it happens fast, modifying social structures and/or organizational processes. It affects norms, interpretive schemes, and resources of the group in significant ways as training progresses. This is the way to focus training on the need for and existence of shared understanding where all team members openly discuss skill development.

Course Description

The training course is geared to creating Motivationally Intelligent Teams using *The RFL Process.*

Organizations that use the process should benefit from featuring full-range communications with feedback and a foundation of partnerships that pursue team and individual goals with equal importance. Organizations should recognize the need to find a balance with individual goals. The resulting training approach teaches coaching, which involves asking open questions, enabling self-discovery, dispelling false feelings and beliefs, addressing changing situations, and looking to the future.

The training also teaches mentoring, which is about answering direct questions, providing information sources, seeking alternative answers, providing structure when needed, and considering the relevance of past experiences. The approach is based on a belief that there is a need to change the focus of training from the traditional leader-centric philosophy to one of engagement, interaction, and collaboration. This creates an atmosphere where leaders and those they lead have equal opportunities to affect the leader-follower relationship that is required in effective teams because they have the benefit of receiving training and resources in interactive, collaborative sessions.

Training objectives include:

- Define and apply *The RFL Process.*
- Define EI and list its attributes.
- Define empathy and list its types.
- Define and apply Engaged Interaction.
- Understand and apply LMX Theory.
- Understand and apply Situational Leadership Theory.
- Identify or develop personal leadership style through self-assessment.
- Assess leader issues of accountability and responsiveness to worker needs.

Training Background

Leaders always need new ways to inspire and motivate people. The motivationally intelligent leader employs Engaged Interaction, EI, and other resources to foster effective workplace communication and relationships. This work goes beyond leadership and management "how to" by offering improved emotional communication that results in new and powerful workplace interactions. The key editorial points are that leaders need certain skills with which they must create a partnership with their team members in a shared vision and a stress-reduced environment.

Combining EI and Engaged Interaction enables connected communications between leaders and the team. Connected communications are about face-to-face, routine discussions with those you lead and supervise. It is important to stay connected with what they are doing, why they are doing it, and how they decide on what activity is necessary. There are three management considerations here: (1) determine the process for getting the work done; (2) establish a way to evaluate and improve the process if necessary; and (3) develop or evolve leadership styles that foster good employee communications. This is done through the skill-building in situational leadership that is part of *The RFL Process*.

Through training, teams can understand that connected communications are the method that facilitates satisfaction of the three management considerations. Leaders must also empower their team members by defining roles and responsibilities. Team members tend to move through the roles of leader, supervisor, and team member based on the task at hand. For instance, before making a substantial change in the organization, the leader should step into the team member's shoes and ask, "Why should they take my advice or use my solution?" The answer should not be, "Because I'm the boss." Through training, the leader should find the common benefit to the organization and person. Supervisors and managers may have the toughest job, because there's a need to envision being able to serve effectively in all three roles.

Good organizational dynamics start with ensuring active listening that uses effective techniques such as questioning, paraphrasing, and summarizing to get out ideas. Energizing every member of the team means modeling the appropriate behavior to establish positive norms, create freedom of expression in team members, and ensure clear expectations throughout the organization. Organizations that allow style diversity in their people can benefit from open and creative culture and collaboration. By also encouraging ongoing self-assessment by all is a way to determine how well the team is functioning and to understand anything that might interfere with effectiveness.

The training will require team projects with a progression of skills and will also feature changing team roles as trainees progress through the program. For instance, the "track" might follow this problem-solving approach.

1. Mini-Paper 1 is a team discussion with a leader, a briefer, and a note taker as defined roles. The briefer will be responsible for reporting the group's results.

2. Mini-Paper 2 is a team discussion with a leader, a briefer, and a note taker as defined roles, but the people in these roles cannot be the same as in Mini-Paper 1. The briefer will be responsible for reporting the group's results.

3. Research Paper is an instructor-approved topic where each member of the team contributes a paragraph or two with their personal evaluation of the topic. Then, the team works together to create an executive summary that can be briefed in about 3 minutes. There is a moderator for the discussion, a briefer, and a note taker as defined roles, but the people in these roles cannot be the same as in Mini-Paper 1 or 2. The briefer will be responsible for reporting the group's results.

Plans

See the next pages for plans that can make a training session or a college course a reality. Right Fit Communications LLC can provide other plans on demand: http://www.rightfitcomm.com/.

RIGHT FIT COMMUNICATIONS, LLC
TEACHING PLAN

The Right Fit Leading (RFL) Process

OPTIONAL TEXT: New RFL Process Develops Leaders and Teams Simultaneously

OVERVIEW: One cannot develop leadership by only focusing on the leader and which of their skills need development or improvement. Using Leader-Member Exchange (LMX) Theory, you can understand that leadership development is best done by developing and/or improving the skills of both the leader and those they lead. This approach leads to shared understanding that allows effective team building. The Right Fit Leading (RFL) Process addresses this challenge.

RFL characterizes leader and team development in terms of three key components. Good leadership and followership are tied to each other, whether they are taught and trained that way or not. Current research supports the belief that good leadership is about philosophy, inspiration, and motivation. The RFL Process is based on emotional intelligence and empathy for all members of any team, regardless of their position or level of responsibility.

The RFL Process addresses a consistent *philosophy* of how we lead and follow. It suggests that we must *inspire* ourselves and others. It also demonstrates the need to *motivate* ourselves and others to take on challenges that we might not attempt otherwise.

Students will be able to:

1) Define and apply the RFL Process
2) Define emotional intelligence (EI) and list its attributes.
3) Define empathy and list its types.
4) Identify effective leadership behavior.
5) Identify and apply Leader-Member Exchange (LMX) Theory.
6) Evaluate different approaches to leadership in organizations.
7) Identify or develop personal leadership style through self-assessment.
8) Assess leader issues of accountability and responsiveness to worker needs.
9) Define and apply engaged interaction:
   a. Create strong relationships where leaders and members interact and achieve shared understanding.
   b. Engaged Interaction is focusing on listening, hearing, and understanding, and continue for as long as it takes.
   c. Understand benefits and flexibility in applying emotional intelligence and empathy to create effective work relationships.
   d. Focus on creating an interactive communication approach that leverages the skills and abilities of all team members and promotes contributions from everyone.

RIGHT FIT COMMUNICATIONS, LLC
TEACHING PLAN

Emotional Intelligence (EI) at Work

OPTIONAL TEXT: TBD

OVERVIEW: Emotional Intelligence is critical for career success. It helps leaders build a collaborative culture, emphasize everyone's strengths, and work to improve weaknesses. The smartest leaders can benefit from EI by finding the best way to create a bond with their team. These leaders use EI to create working relationships that allow the best and brightest on the team to share their technical expertise with solid recommendations for action

Students will be able to:

1) Define emotional intelligence (EI) and list its attributes.
2) Define empathy and list its types.
3) Identify effective leadership behavior.
4) Identify and apply Leader-Member Exchange (LMX) Theory.
5) Evaluate different approaches to leadership in organizations.
6) Identify or develop personal leadership style through self-assessment.
7) Assess leader issues of accountability and responsiveness to worker needs.

Promote engaged interaction:
- Create strong relationships where leaders and members interact and achieve shared understanding.
- Engaged interaction is focusing on listening, hearing, and understanding, and continue for as long as it takes.
- Understand benefits and flexibility in applying emotional intelligence and empathy to create effective work relationships.
- Focus on creating an interactive communication approach that leverages the skills and abilities of all team members and promotes contributions from everyone.

REFERENCE: (Brown Sr, 2021, p. Chapter 7)

EXPERIMENTAL AND CLINICAL PSYCHOLOGY:

The RFL Process has some foundation in the writings of T.A. Ryan and P.C. Smith (1954), who argued for new paradigms of experimental and clinical psychology. They argued that it was useless and misleading to try to translate worker goals into the 1925 argument of Watson concerning stimuli and responses. The difficulty, they argued, was that Watson's assertion implies that the laws that govern these stimuli and responses in experimental laboratory paradigms are the same as those that hold for all other stimuli and responses in everyday situations. They argued, instead, for a focus on the wants, wishes, desires, and experiences of the individual.

BEHAVIORISM:

This work uses behaviorism as a foundation for engagement and training efforts. B.F. Skinner (1966) asserted that changes in behavior are the result of an individual's response to events (stimuli) that occur in the environment. A response produces a consequence such as defining a word, hitting a ball, or solving a math problem. Skinner analyzed Stimulus-Response (S-R) patterns, arguing that when a particular S-R pattern is reinforced (rewarded), the individual is conditioned to respond. Reinforcement is the key, and a reinforcer is anything that strengthens the desired response.

LMX THEORY:

LMX addresses, in part, intentions on the part of participants in work relationships. We can learn more by studying Edwin Locke, who was an ardent critic of behaviorism. His 1964 doctoral dissertation was based on experiments testing Ryan's hypothesis regarding the effect of intentions. Latham recounts the results (1965).

The culmination of Locke's experiments led to three propositions that would subsequently lead to the development of goal setting theory in 1990: (1) Specific high goals lead to higher performance than no goals or even an abstract goal such as "do your best"; (2) given goal commitment, the higher the goal the higher the performance, and (3) variables such as monetary incentives, participation in decision making, feedback, or knowledge of results affect performance only to the extent that they lead to the setting of and commitment to specific high goals. In short, goals have the effect of directing attention and action *(choice)*, mobilizing energy expenditure or *effort*, prolonging effort over time *(persistence)*, and motivating the individual to develop relevant strategies *(cognition)* for goal attainment. Given goal commitment, job performance improves because the goal provides a regulatory mechanism that allows the employee to observe, monitor, subjectively evaluate, and adjust job behavior to attain the goal. Goal setting taps a fundamental attribute of human behavior, namely, goal directedness (Latham, 2012, pp. 53-54).

GOAL SETTING AND EQUITY:

When we think about team dynamics, it is often about how people are treated AND how they think they are treated. C.A. O'Reilly (1991) found that the majority of organizational behavior studies focus on the dominant theories of goal setting and equity. Latham advances the notion that organizational justice principles are as much about leadership as they are about employee motivation. There are two considerations: (1) Distributive justice focuses on what was distributed, who it was distributed to, and who received what distribution; and (2) Procedural justice is concerned with whether there are procedures, processes, or systems in place for determining what was distributed to whom.

MOTIVATIONAL INTELLIGENCE & SOCIOANALYTIC THEORY:

Motivationally intelligent leaders should always be interested in what motivates their team. Robert and Joyce Hogan developed Socioanalytic Theory (2001). The theory asserts that people are constantly in need of either getting along or getting ahead. They are pursuing getting along when they pursue acceptance, approval, and popularity. Getting ahead involves the need for power, control, and status. Interpersonal relationships are inherently problematic because of the dichotomy of actions. One can solve the problem of getting along by simply acting in a way that would avoid disapproval. However, to get ahead one may need to adopt more active and manipulative forms of self-presentation.

NEED THEORIES:

Knowing the members of your team and what motivates them is always important. Abraham Maslow argued that as one need is fulfilled, its strength is diminished and the strength of the next need in the hierarchy is increased. Maslow's theory had a tremendous influence on Douglas McGregor's Theory X and Theory Y (1960). McGregor viewed himself as a behavioral scientist and advanced the notion in 1957 that it was time to apply social sciences to make human organizations truly effective. McGregor based his argument on assumptions about motivation. There were criticisms that McGregor did not have enough data, but he still made assumptions about human motivation that leads to two approaches.

Theory X: People inherently dislike work, they must be coerced or controlled to do work to achieve objectives, and they prefer to be directed.

Theory Y: People will exercise self-direction and self-control towards achieving objectives they are committed to, and people will learn to accept and seek responsibility.

Ayoko, O. B., Härtel, C. E., & Callan, V. J. (2002). Resolving the puzzle of productive and destructive conflict in culturally heterogeneous workgroups: A communication accommodation theory approach. *International Journal of Conflict Management, 13*(2), 165-195.

Bates, C. (2016). A methodology study of Hersey and Blanchard situational leadership theory. *Int J Adv Eng Technol Manage Appl Sci, 3*(11), 42-48.

Beauregard, T. A., Basile, K. A., & Canonico, E. (2019). Telework: outcomes and facilitators for employees.

Brown, M. A., Sr. (2017). *Solutions for High-Touch Communications in a High-Tech World*. Hershey, PA, USA: IGI Global.

Brown, M. A., Sr. (2021). *3D Coaching: Suggestions for a New Approach*: Right Fit Communications LLC.

Brown Sr, M. A. (2017). *Motivationally Intelligent Leadership: Emerging Research and Opportunities: Emerging Research and Opportunities*: IGI Global.

Brown Sr, M. A. (2021). *Analyzing Telework, Trustworthiness, and Performance Using Leader-Member Exchange: COVID-19 Perspective: COVID-19 Perspective*: IGI Global.

Brown Sr., M. A. (2021). *Analyzing Telework, Trustworthiness, and Performance Using Leader-Member Exchange: COVID-19 Perspective: COVID-19 Perspective*: IGI Global.

Daft, R. L., & Macintosh, N. B. (1981). A Tentative Exploration into the Amount and Equivocality of Information Processing in Organizational Work Units. *Administrative Science Quarterly, 26*(2), 207-224.

Dalal, A. (2017). An Exploratory Study on Conflict Management with the Perspective of Education as a Variable. *Australian Academy of Business and Economics Review, 3*(1), 13-26.

De Meyer, A. (2011). Collaborative leadership: New perspectives in leadership development. *The Future of Leadership Development: Corporate Needs and the Role of Business Schools*, 44-63.

Deshwal, V., & Ali, M. A. (2020). A systematic review of various leadership theories. *Shanlax International Journal of Commerce, 8*(1), 38-43.

DiMicco, J. M., & Millen, D. R. (2008, April 5-10, 2008). *People Sensemaking with Social Networking Sites*. Paper presented at the Sensemaking Workshop, CHI 2008, Florence, Italy.

Frank Messina, E. D. (2011). *Two-And-A-Half Minutes To "Effective": Daily Thoughts for Improving Your Effectiveness in the Areas of Communications, Coaching, and Delegation*: Xlibris US.

Gallois, C., & Giles, H. (2015). Communication Accommodation Theory *The International Encyclopedia of Language and Social Interaction*: John Wiley & Sons, Inc.

Gallup, I. (2017). State of the American workplace. *Pobrane z http://www. gallup. com/reports/199961/state-american-workplace-report-2017. aspx.*

Giles, H. (2008). *Communication accommodation theory*: Sage Publications, Inc.

Granovetter, M. S. (1973). The Strength of Weak Ties. *The American Journal of Sociology, 78*(6), 1360-1380.

Hogan, R., & Hogan, J. (2001). Assessing leadership: A view from the dark side. *International Journal of Selection and assessment, 9*(1-2), 40-51.

Janse, B. (2019). Leader-Member Exchange Theory (LMX). *Toolshero*. Retrieved from Retrieved May 11,2021: https://www.toolshero.com/management/leader-member-exchange-theory-lmx/

Jones, L., Woodhouse, D., & Rowe, J. (2007). Effective nurse parent communication: a study of parents' perceptions in the NICU environment. *Patient education and counseling, 69*(1), 206-212.

Latham, G. P. (2007). *Work motivation: history, theory, research, and practice*. Thousand Oaks, Calif.: Sage Publications.

Latham, G. P. (2012). *Work motivation: History, theory, research, and practice*: Sage.

Latham, G. P., & Budworth, M.-H. (2007). The Study of Work Motivation in the 20th Century.

Leclercq-Vandelannoitte, A., & Isaac, H. (2016). The new office: how coworking changes the work concept. *Journal of Business Strategy, 37*(6), 3-9. doi:doi:10.1108/JBS-10-2015-0105

Leinonen, P., Järvelä, S., & Häkkinen, P. (2005). Conceptualizing the Awareness of Collaboration: A Qualitative Study of a Global Virtual Team. *Comput Supported Coop Work Computer Supported Cooperative Work (CSCW), 14*(4), 301-322.

Locke, E. A. (1965). Interaction of ability and motivation in performance. *Perceptual and Motor Skills, 21*(3), 719-725.

Maslow, A. H. (1970). *Motivation and personality*. New York: Harper & Row.

McGregor, D. (1960a). Theory X and theory Y. *Organization theory, 358*(1), 374.

McGregor, D. (1960b). Theory X and theory Y. *Organization theory*, 358-374.

Mills, J. H., & Mills, A. J. (2000). *Sensemaking and the Gendering of Organizational Culture*. Paper presented at the ASAC-IFSAM Conference, Montreal, Quebec, Canada.

Mowday, R. T., Steers, R. M., & Porter, L. W. (1979). The measurement of organizational commitment. *Journal of vocational behavior, 14*(2), 224-247.

Nardi, B. A., & Whittaker, S. (2002). The place of face-to-face communication in distributed work. *Distributed work,* 83-110.

O'Reilly III, C. A. (1991). Organizational behavior: Where we've been, where we're going. *Annual Review of Psychology, 42*(1), 427-458.

O'Daniel, M., & Rosenstein, A. H. (2008). Professional Communication and Team Collaboration. In R. G. Hughes (Ed.), Patient Safety and Quality: An Evidence-Based Handbook for Nurses. Rockville (MD): Agency for Healthcare Research and Quality (US). Retrieved from https://www.ncbi.nlm.nih.gov/books/NBK2637/.

Perrow, C. (1967). A Framework for the Comparative Analysis of Organizations. *American Sociological Review, 32*(2), 194-208.

Porter, C. E., & Donthu, N. (2008). Cultivating Trust and Harvesting Value in Virtual Communities. *Management Science, 54*(1), 113-128. doi:10.1287/mnsc.1070.0765

Porter, M. E. (2008). The five competitive forces that shape strategy. *Harvard business review, 86*(1), 25-40.

Rawlins, C., & Wilson, H. (1996). *Introduction to management.* London: Harper-CollinsPublishers.

Roberts, K. H., & O'Reilly III, C. A. (1973). *Some problems in measuring organizational communication.* Retrieved from

Ryan, T. A., & Smith, P. C. (1954). Principles of industrial psychology.

Skinner, B. F. (1966). What is the experimental analysis of behavior? *Journal of the Experimental Analysis of behavior, 9*(3), 213.

Stets, J. E. (1991). Psychological aggression in dating relationships: The role of interpersonal control. *Journal of Family Violence, 6*(1), 97-114.

Stillman, J. (2012). Do Bosses and Employees See Eye to Eye on Anything? *Inc.com.* Retrieved from https://www.inc.com/jessica-stillman/do-bosses-and-employee-see-eye-to-eye-on-anything.html

Thompson, G., & Glasø, L. (2015). Situational leadership theory: A test from three perspectives. *Leadership & Organization Development Journal, 36*(5), 527-544.

Tuckman, B. W., & Jensen, M. A. C. (2010). Stages of small-group development Revisited1. *Group Facilitation*(10), 43.

Tushman, M. L., & Nadler, D. A. (1978). Information processing as an integrating concept in organizational design. *Academy of management review, 3*(3), 613-624.

Welker, G. A. (2004). *Patterns of order processing: a study of the formalization of the ordering process in order-driven manufacturing companies.* University of Groningen.

Wellman, B. (1997). An electronic group is virtually a social network. In S. Kiesler (Ed.), *Culture of the Internet* (pp. 179-205). Hillsdale, N.J.: Lawrence Erlbaum.

Wellman, B., & Wortley, S. (1990). Different Strokes from Different Folks: Community Ties and Social Support. *The American Journal of Sociology, 96*(3), 558-588.

Withey, M., Daft, R. L., & Cooper, W. H. (1983). Measures of Perrow's Work Unit Technology: An Empirical Assessment and a New Scale. *The Academy of Management Journal, 26*(1), 45-63.